Praise for *The Mindfulness Toolbox*

"This is a must-have book for every therapist using mindfulness approaches with clients. From the 10 'Tips' thru the 40 'Tools', Donald Altman shares his considerable wisdom, along with a sense of respect for both the client—and the therapist. At the same time, the material is presented in a light and very usable style, from the clear outlines to the many client handouts."

—**Jean L. Kristeller, Ph.D., Research and clinical psychologist, and developer of Mindfulness-Based Eating Awareness Training (MB-EAT)**

"The ceaselessly creative Donald Altman, in his never-ending quest to make mindfulness practice accessible to anyone motivated to learn it, has once again broached new ground in elaborating simple, useful techniques for applying mindfulness in everyday life. *The Mindfulness Toolbox* is a veritable wonderland of user-friendly implements of mindfulness practice, all laid out to maximize a new (and maybe not-so-new) practitioner's ability to effectively use applied mindfulness. *The Mindfulness Toolbox* will be a tremendous aid and benefit to all people who practice and teach mindfulness."

—**Jeffrey M. Schwartz, MD, author of *Brain Lock and You Are Not Your Brain***

"Much like any healing prescription, *The Mindfulness Toolbox* skillfully reduces pain and fosters balance by getting to the root cause of the symptoms. If you want to expand your mindfulness repertoire, you won't find a more complete and practical set of key techniques, handouts, and ideas. You'll even be guided as to which tools fit together, such as tools for sensing the body, tools for meditation, and tools for getting into the present moment. With a large dose of awareness, clarity, precision, simplicity, and insight, Donald Altman has given us a potent and worthwhile medicine for inviting well-being, acceptance, and inner peace."

—**Paul Harrison, creator and producer of The Mindfulness Movie, and author of *Where's My Zen?* and *The Ten Paradoxes: The Science of Where's My Zen?***

"Mindfulness has swept through the mental health profession in the past several decades and plays a major role in important modalities such as DBT, ACT, Mindfulness-Based Cognitive Therapy for Depression, Mindfulness-Based Relapse Prevention and others. Whether or not you are trained in any of these modalities, *The Mindfulness Toolbox* by Donald Altman is the resource you need to strengthen your use of mindfulness with a wide variety of clients. Altman is an experienced and loving guide to lead you through the mindfulness landscape. His new book presents a comprehensive set of highly practical, effective techniques, tools and handouts that will enable you to skillfully utilize mindfulness in your clinical work. The easy-to-use interventions for anxiety, depression, stress and pain are described in clear language that reflects the kindness and beauty of mindfulness. *The Mindfulness Toolbox* will not only improve your effectiveness with clients, it will also enable you to more fully integrate into your personal life the emotional, psychological and spiritual wealth offered by mindfulness practice. If you have any interest in mindfulness, you should have *The Mindfulness Toolbox* as a resource."

—**Terry Fralich, LPC, JD, author of *The Five Core Skills of Mindfulness* and *Cultivating Lasting Happiness***

"*The Mindfulness Toolbox* is a treasure trove of resources for healing and belongs in every clinician's office. It teaches simple, effective ways to reduce suffering and increase happiness. Well worth reading!"

—**Mary NurrieStearns, author of *Yoga For Anxiety, Yoga For Emotional Trauma,* and *Yoga Mind, Peaceful Mind***

THE MINDFULNESS TOOLBOX

*50 Practical Mindfulness Tips, Tools, and Handouts
for Anxiety, Depression, Stress, and Pain*

by

DONALD ALTMAN, M.A., LPC

Published by
PESI Publishing & Media
PESI, Inc.
3839 White Ave
Eau Claire, WI 54703
www.pesipublishing.com

Cover Design: Matt Pabich
Layout Design: Bookmasters
Edited By: Marietta Whittlesey & Catherine Bernstein

Printed in the United States of America

ISBN: 978-1-9361288-6-0

PESI
Publishing
& Media
www.pesipublishing.com

This book is dedicated to peace
and all who seek peace,
within and without.

May each grain of mindfulness
be a blessing of awakening
on behalf of all who suffer.

May each grain of mindfulness
be an instrument of peace and love
for the benefit and well-being of all.

About the Author

Donald Altman, M.A., LPC is a psychotherapist, award-winning writer, former Buddhist monk, and adjunct faculty at *Portland State University*. A featured expert in *The Mindfulness Movie*, he is the author of several pioneering books on how to integrate ancient mindfulness into modern life, including *One-Minute Mindfulness, The Mindfulness Code, The Joy Compass, Living-Kindness, Art of the Inner Meal, and 12-Weeks to Mindful Eating.* Donald has served as Vice-President of *The Center for Mindful Eating* and conducts mindfulness workshops nationally.

Table of Contents

Section 1 – Essential Mindfulness Tips for Therapists

Section 2 – Mindfulness Tools for Anxiety

Section 3 – Mindfulness Tools for Depression

Section 4 – Mindfulness Tools for Stress

Section 5 – Mindfulness Tools for Pain

Acknowledgments

My deepest gratitude extends to all those individuals who have dedicated themselves to sharing with others the teachings of peace and mindfulness. I want to thank my late teacher, the Venerable U. Sīlānanda; Ashin Thitzana, U. Thondara, and the monks and community of the Burma Buddhist Monastery; Randy Fitzgerald, Greg Crosby, Paul Harrison, Lama Surya Das, and Jeff Schwartz, friends journeying the mindfulness path who offered useful ideas and reflections; Linda Jackson, publisher at PESI Publishing & Media, for bringing a joyful enthusiasm and a collaborative spirit to this project; I am also very grateful for numerous others at PESI/CMI who helped to pave the way for this project by getting me on the road to teach mindfulness across the country—Marnie Sullivan, Anna Fisher, Mike Olson, Shannon Becker, Geri Steinke, and others; also, PPM's creative design team and editor Marietta Whittlesey.

Finally, this book would not have been possible without numerous friends, associates, colleagues, clients, workshop participants, and others—who helped me explore, practice, and deepen mindfulness each day. I am especially indebted to my mother, Barbara, for her gentle spirit and love, and to my entire family for the priceless lessons in mindfulness that I got free of charge!

Introduction

Given today's technology and medicine, I don't think anyone would choose to switch places with our ancestors. And yet, the statistics related to the percentage of those struggling with clinically diagnosable anxiety and depression are truly staggering. Add to that the number of people suffering from stress-related physical and emotional issues—a number that the American Psychological Association reports as almost seven in ten persons. Then, there are those who are distraught and unable to find abiding peace because of painful conditions, whether chronic or temporary.

Why is this pandemic of suffering so pervasive? Teacher and author J. Krishnamurti once advised, "It is no measure of health to be well adjusted to a profoundly sick society." Rather than focus on the symptoms—the visible signs of *dis-ease*—it can be a worthwhile endeavor to investigate the root causes of emotional dysregulation and imbalance. Trying to fix only the symptoms is like the homeowner who paints over a water-stained wall in the living room without looking into the actual cause of the leak. The paint may look nice and cover up the problem for a while, but the water stain will eventually reappear and more damage will be done to the building's infrastructure.

As social and holistic beings with a hundred billion neurons in our brains, we are far too complex for simplistic answers. We need to look more deeply, and we can attempt this by considering the entire environment with which we interact. That's where mindfulness comes into the picture. Mindfulness is an approach for directly confronting those difficult questions and situations that arrive at our doorstep each day. Instead of shielding us from uncomfortable truths, mindfulness pinches us gently, but firmly—reminding us to awaken to the way things are, which is a stable and valuable vantage point from which to cultivate change. What is more, the experience of mindfulness runs the gamut from the micro to the macro—from sensate-focusing to an expansive, transpersonal consciousness.

One central theme that runs throughout *The Mindfulness Toolbox* is this: *You can only change that which you are first aware of.* Mindfulness empowers those who practice it because it offers freedom of choice. It can dramatically alter *how* we experience the daily stress pollutants of chaos, confusion, loss, anger, grief, and fear that confront every human. In what is probably one of the most transitional periods in history, mindfulness is a life preserver of resilience that keeps us afloat and invites the healing salves of acceptance and compassion. Fundamentally, it brings us into greater balance with both the stressful external world and our internal experience of mind, body, and thoughts. **Mindfulness is a powerful, scientifically proven medicine for breaking free from harmful emotional ruts and mindless habits in order to live with full awareness and greater freedom.**

WHY THE MINDFULNESS TOOLBOX

The idea and vision behind *The Mindfulness Toolbox* is to offer therapists a comprehensive set of highly practical, effective handouts and tools—not found elsewhere in any one source—for helping clients deal with a wide range of issues. Whether you need effective handouts and tools for pain, stress, anxiety, or depression, they can be found in this book. This approach also integrates the latest in brain research, whose findings are very compatible with mindfulness. Neuroscience has demonstrated that where and how we place our attention, the very thoughts we have, and even how we observe our breath, can change the physical structure of the brain— as well as alter hundreds of biological processes in the body.

Mindful awareness invites a very different kind of awareness, one that dramatically alters our *experience* of that depression, that anxious thought, that sensation of pain, or that stressful event. This new experience breaks old mindsets and maladaptive coping mechanisms, as well as rewires the brain's neural pathways. Sometimes, this allows for a whole new meaning or understanding to evolve around one's difficulties. At other times, it stimulates the growth of personal wisdom through which a more accepting, less self-critical, and open perspective takes root.

While this book is based on many core mindfulness concepts, the handouts and practices are not meant to be a step-by-step training in mindfulness. Rather, they are targeted interventions that put to use basic mindfulness practices of breath awareness, mind and thought awareness, and body-movement awareness. These concepts do not even need to be presented as "mindfulness" tools or practices. As explored in Tip #1, *Expanding Your Mindfulness Vocabulary*, it is always a good idea to adapt your description of mindfulness in a way that clients can best understand it.

As you guide clients through material in this book, some may express the desire to learn more about mindfulness or seek to become a serious mindfulness student. (This is not unusual, because practicing mindfulness is like eating a potato chip—you enjoy it so much that you can't stop after having just one). For motivated individuals, there are many ways to guide them toward a more systematic practice of mindfulness. There exist many in-person trainings at local mindfulness centers or retreat centers—many of which can be found on the Internet. There are also instructional courses, such as my own guidebook, *A Course in Mindfulness*, a self-paced instructional workbook that includes guided audio meditations (see **Bibliography/References**).

In addition to tuning in to the delicate rhythms of one's mind and body, there is yet another important benefit to this persistent, gentle path of greater presence and awakening. These practices inevitably get clients out of themselves and closer to the truth of the connectedness between all living things. Mindfulness sparks what I like to call *We-Thou* awareness. This is similar to what Martin Buber called the *I-Thou* relationship, and what Buddhist monk and author Thich Nhat Hanh has referred to as our state of *interbeing*. This shift from *I* to *We* is more than a major shift in perspective. It is a paradigm shift toward transpersonal awareness.

What does this mean? By cultivating *We-Thou* awareness, individuals can get free from the often limited, distorted, and narrow *I-centric* view of life that entraps them. From the *I-centric* perspective, others are seen as separate and isolated *objects* that must be moved about and manipulated like chess pieces in order to stay safe and survive in a dangerous world. Defending the *I-centric* view leads to isolation, pain, and suffering because it fosters fear and mistrust. In contrast, the *We-Thou* perspective encourages sustainable, long-lasting and loving relationships with others, as well as with all living beings and 'mother' Earth that supports us all. It promotes a compassionate viewpoint and the understanding that all persons have suffered in some way.

After all, don't all humans—indeed, all living beings—seek to feel safe, healthy, peaceful, and secure? **In sum, mindfulness benefits and empowers clients by providing them with the skills necessary to gain a broader understanding, acceptance, and sense of compassion for themselves and their situation.**

HOW TO USE THIS BOOK AND ITS FOUR KEY FEATURES

There is no single way to use this book. If you have clients with particular issues, it's simple to refer to the *Table of Contents* to find the Section you're interested in: *Mindfulness Tools for Anxiety, Mindfulness Tools for Depression, Mindfulness Tools for Stress,* and *Mindfulness Tools for Pain*. There you will find brief descriptions of the interventions. First, however, it will help to understand the four unique features of *The Mindfulness Toolbox* and the handouts it contains.

The first of these unique features is Section 1 – ***Mindfulness Tips for Therapists***. Begin by reviewing this introductory section, even if you find a specific mindfulness intervention that you want to use with a client. This section provides general tips and ideas that can make your treatment more effective. It lays the groundwork for increasing your own understanding of mindfulness, as well as helping clients to clearly see the benefits. Section 1 also features several handouts for clients. In addition, each individual chapter, or 'Tool,' contains its own bulleted *Tips for Working with Clients* which target issues specifically related to that intervention.

The second unique feature is the ***integration of learning styles***. By understanding a client's learning style, you can tap into how this individual most readily "gets" or learns new information. There are nine different learning styles listed and explained in Tip #3, *Tapping into a Client's Learning Style*. It can be helpful to get familiar with these. If a client possesses an especially strong visual learning style, for example, you may decide to start with a visual-oriented mindfulness practice over one that focuses on hearing or the body. One of the first things you'll see at the top of each chapter, or Tool, is a list of learning styles that fit with that tool. A quick glance at this list will save you time by more accurately identifying a practice that works best for that client, and the client will feel more understood.

The third unique feature of this guidebook is that several of the handouts are written as ***readable scripts*** that you can use as guided meditations during a therapy session. In this way, you can directly guide clients through the practice for the very first time. You also have the option of recording the script for those clients who find it helpful to hear the words guiding them.

The fourth special feature is that ***closely related Tools are cross-referenced throughout*** and can be grouped together. For example, there are many different ways to drop into the body as a sensate-focusing practice—sometimes the emphasis may be on pain; at other times it may be on anxiety or on depression. While each has a slightly different focus, complementary practices can be grouped together for clients. To quickly find which practices can be bundled together, just look at the bullet-pointed *Tips for Working with Clients* section. This cross-referencing provides clients with a broader range of concepts to work with, as well as deepening their understanding of a particular topic, or practice.

In addition to the above-mentioned features, *The Mindfulness Toolbox* contains specialized writing areas for *Reflections* throughout. This offers clients the perfect place to journal and process their experiences. Included are many follow-up questions and homework for daily practice. These can easily be used to help track a client's progress and to help clients use the skills on a more consistent basis. **The four special features in this book will give you a roadmap**

and concrete methods for working with clients while employing mindfulness skills that can be used over and over again.

It is my hope that this book contributes to bringing more wellness and balance into the lives of those you are working with. May you continue the journey of reducing suffering and changing lives for the better.

Section 1

ESSENTIAL MINDFULNESS TIPS FOR THERAPISTS

Tip #1
Expanding the Mindfulness Vocabulary

THOUGHTS FOR THERAPISTS

Have you ever mentioned the word *meditation* or *mindful* to a client, only to be greeted by a panicked expression or negative response?

There are a great many people who would benefit from a mindfulness practice for reducing pain, anxiety, depression, or stress. Sometimes, however, an individual may have a history or personal religious background that acts as a negative filter that blocks them from opening up to such practices. When this occurs, it helps to be prepared with a broader and more expansive mindfulness vocabulary—one that doesn't depend on words like *mindfulness* or *meditation*.

By expanding your mindfulness vocabulary, you might find a wonderful and creative way to enter a client's world. Sometimes it could be a metaphor for mindfulness or meditation, such as getting in the zone; other times you might simply use another, more generic term, such as paying attention or observing with non-judgment. What follows are some ideas for expanding your vocabulary. Use the ideas below, or let them serve as springboards for enhancing your own personal mindfulness terminology.

MINDFULNESS IN TRADITIONAL VOCABULARY

Historically, the ancient Sanskrit word *sati* was used to define the ability to observe things with a sense of what could be termed *bare awareness*. In other words, just noticing things for what they are without adding or subtracting anything. This means observing thoughts, sensations in the body, and emotions in an impartial and neutral way. Potentially, all of our experiences could be viewed in this way. This can be thought of as a safe way of distancing from negativity or a personal bias. Learning to observe things in this more objective way, of course, takes lots of time, practice, and patience.

MODERN DEFINITIONS FOR MINDFULNESS

So, how can we start to bring this more traditional idea into the modern world and connect with our clients? Below are several ways to describe mindfulness that use concepts that fit with our modern language and sensibility.

- opening to the moment
- noticing the truth of change
- an open-hearted acceptance of this moment
- living in the *what-is* as opposed to the *what-if*
- getting freed from habit and reactivity

- acceptance and letting-go
- focusing on the moment
- changing the history channel
- loving awareness
- tuning-in
- moment-to-moment awareness of the breath
- stop, look, and listen
- non-dual awareness
- unplugging
- finding the center
- prayerfulness
- leaving the busy mind by dropping into the body
- awareness that doesn't take sides
- inner hospitality
- cultivating a neutral, detached awareness

FINDING A BROADER VOCABULARY FOR MINDFULNESS

In travelling around the country and facilitating mindfulness workshops, I've always enjoyed the process that occurs when therapists get into small groups to brainstorm other words or phrases that can be used to help their clients grasp mindfulness. You might notice that some phrases or words work better for a certain population—such as children, people in pain, substance addiction, etc.—while many will work for people in general.

Some of ideas included here are metaphors for sports (*getting in the zone* and *getting into the game*) or how we use technology (*hitting the pause button* and *changing the channel*). What follows is a useful handout that can help patients identify the word or phrase that works best for them. Everyone has a different sensibility and learning style that will help to find the right terminology, image, or metaphor. Have fun working with clients as they explore options that you can use and adapt together.

CONCLUSIONS

Having the right mindfulness vocabulary—one that fits the client—can create a bridge and build the therapeutic relationship. This is a creative process, and the client may or may not use the exact words from the handout. For example, in the sports film *For the Love of the Game*, the main character (a baseball pitcher played by Kevin Costner) uses a mindfulness practice that he calls *clear the mechanism* in order to block out all distractions, get totally focused, and ready to pitch!

The handout is a starting point from which to broaden and explore mindfulness. Keep in mind, too, that visual imagery—such as a soothing color—as well as physical movement or gestures can be another way to access mindfulness. In addition, the words someone uses may also be a clue as to what mindfulness practices they will find most useful.

HANDOUT: GETTING INTO THE PRESENT MOMENT

Instructions: There are many words to use when thinking about getting into the present moment. This handout contains many different words and phrases to describe how to think about leaving stress, anxiety, and negative thoughts behind.

Look over this list and find what words or phrases connect with you. Or, you might come up with your own words that help you connect with being calm and present. Use this list as a starting point. **Circle the words or phrases that you like the best.**

- chill-axin'
- getting into the game
- hitting the pause button
- in the eye of the hurricane
- clarity
- impartial witness/spectator
- coming back to your senses
- be here now
- the present moment
- making friends with your mind
- watching and observing
- curiosity; being curious
- picturing the ocean or a river
- changing your relationship to thoughts and feelings
- putting on the right gear for stormy weather

- getting in the zone
- getting in touch
- patience
- peace, calm, and stillness
- taking a breath
- changing the channel
- focused attention
- surfing the moment
- in the flow
- non-judging awareness
- non-blaming; openness
- acceptance of this moment
- creating space (from negativity)

Reflections: If you have other words or phrases not listed above, write these here:

_____.
_____.

_____.

What is an example of a good time and place that you could put your favorite word or words to use?

_____.

_____.

What do you see as the biggest challenge you will face when trying to use your word or phrase for getting in the present moment?_____.

_____.

_____.

Tip #2
Making Mindfulness Effective

THOUGHTS FOR THERAPISTS

It is very common for anyone learning mindfulness to have a running commentary in her or his head that might be admonishing them with thoughts like, *I'm not doing this right, I'll never do this perfectly*, or *I'm a failure because I can't stop my thoughts, so I might as well give up!* Even the most experienced meditation and mindfulness practitioners—and you may be one of them—know how such self-critical thoughts can derail a mindfulness practice.

The key here is to let clients know that they don't have to be perfect with these practices. Like any skill, mindfulness requires time and patience to learn it well. By directly addressing this issue, you can normalize the challenges faced by someone learning to notice the breath, the body, or the mind with focused attention. Mark Twain addressed this challenge when he said:

> *It's easy to give up smoking.*
> *I know because I've done it thousands of times.*

The same could be said about mindfulness:

> *It's easy to remember to practice mindfulness.*
> *I know because I've reminded myself to do it thousands of times.*

ASK CLIENTS 'THE 3-MINUTE QUESTION'

One way to reframe a mindfulness practice is to put it in the context of daily self-care. This includes asking clients what I refer to as *The 3-Minute Question*. This question can be posed as follows:

> *During the day, you spend several minutes taking care of your physical body and physical hygiene. This includes things like taking a shower, brushing your teeth, even getting dressed in the morning.*
> *But what about spending even a few minutes working on your mental hygiene? Are you worth 3-minutes a day taking care of your mind and brain with a daily mindfulness hygiene practice? This is about the same amount of time you might spend brushing your teeth. So ask yourself: "Am I worth 3 minutes a day?"*

TIPS FOR WORKING WITH CLIENTS

After you teach the clients a mindfulness practice, use the handout and the story below to illustrate that "there is no being perfect" when it comes to mindfulness. You can also state the benefits of a mindfulness practice for clients as follows:

- Mindfulness enhances flexibility and adaptability. If an individual has felt stuck and frustrated by old habits, mindfulness skills promote methods for retraining the brain to get off auto-pilot. In other words, mindfulness teaches how to put on the brakes and slow down before acting on an impulse.

- Mindfulness cultivates curiosity and greater ease. It helps one explore the journey and the process, as opposed to being overly focused and worried about the outcome.

- Mindfulness changes one's relationship to self-critical and self-blaming thoughts, thus promoting greater patience, kindness, acceptance, and hospitality toward oneself and others. Mindfulness skills and tools also help to overcome dualistic all-or-none thinking.

- Mindfulness encourages greater fulfillment in daily life by focusing more on the present moment, and by reducing rumination and negative thoughts, as well as anxiety about the future.

HANDOUT: A STORY: PRACTICING MINDFULNESS WITH KINDFULNESS

There was once a mindfulness institute that placed an advertisement in a daily newspaper and in various social media sites. The short ad read as follows:

One-day Enlightenment. Guaranteed. Call: 555-Mindful

A woman saw this ad and got very excited. She had been dealing with daily stressors, a new job, and even health issues. She called to get the address and the very next morning she went to the institute and found one of the instructors.

"I saw your ad. What do you mean by enlightenment?" she asked.

"Clarity of mind," said the instructor. "Also, a sense of peace and inner calm, even in the midst of life's difficulties. All you have to do," he explained, "is to follow your breath completely, noticing the in-breath, the pause, and the out-breath—without any distractions for the next seven hours to realize your goal."

The woman glanced at her wristwatch, smiled and said, "Fabulous, I'll have my enlightenment by dinnertime! Sign me up." She was given a cushion to sit on, and so she began. The first in-breath was fantastic, and she was present with it the entire time. Right then, however, a siren blared outside. The woman's sense of hearing grabbed onto the siren and brought it inside her mind, where it started to spin a story: *That's loud. Don't they know we're trying to get our enlightenment in here?*

Just then she realized she had forgotten about her breath. And so she started again, noticing the complete in-breath and then being present with the pause. She was just starting her out-breath when a fly buzzed by. She opened her eyes and her sense of sight went and grabbed the fly and brought it inside her mind. Again, the mind spun an elaborate story: *I wonder if we're going to have lunch, because having flies isn't a good idea. Maybe someone left the window open. Who should I talk to?* Finally, she remembered about her breath, and so she started again . . . and again. As the story goes, she was still there ten years later trying to get her seven consecutive hours of breath awareness!

That's why mindfulness is more accurately called *re*-mindfulness. It's totally okay to remind yourself to come back to being aware of the mind and body and environment time and time again. Remember, there's no being perfect with mindfulness. You don't have to stop your thoughts, either. Just noticing them is good enough. *In fact, when it comes to learning mindfulness **good enough is always good enough**.* Because mindfulness is *re-mindfulness*, there's never any failure with it. And it's why mindfulness is a way of inviting and practicing kindness toward yourself.

Reflections: If you have critical or distracted thoughts during your mindfulness practice, just notice them, smile inwardly, knowing that by noticing thoughts you are actually doing the practice! Then, just think of the words "good enough" to release the thoughts and return to your practice. Write down your experiences in the space below.

_____

_____

_____

_____

_____

_____

_____

Tip #3
Tapping into a Client's Learning Style

THOUGHTS FOR THERAPISTS

At the beginning of each chapter you will find a list of learning styles that match up well with the mindfulness practice, or intervention, that is featured in that chapter. That's important, because mindfulness is a skill that is most easily learned when it is tailored to fit *how* a particular person learns. It's helpful to recognize that not every mindfulness skill will work equally well for all persons. For example, a highly verbal and linguistically oriented individual will be more attuned to mindfulness practices that are linked to words, thoughts, or storytelling. Likewise, someone who excels at tactile and spatial learning will probably find a mindful walking, yoga, or other movement practice to be more engaging.

Mindfulness methods for reflection and developing focused attention, openness, and acceptance are expressed in a rainbow of shapes and forms. These include sound and chanting, dance and movement, reading, mindfulness, meditation, dialogue, and prayer, to name a few. Notice the broad range of learning styles these incorporate. Fortunately, there are nine different learning styles to help almost anyone find a mindfulness practice that they can connect with and use effectively. And, in many cases, a mindfulness intervention will be appropriate for more than one learning style.

TIPS FOR USING LEARNING STYLE WITH CLIENTS

Often, clients will let you know if a particular practice isn't engaging for them. If you are not sure of a client's learning style or want to investigate learning styles with clients, the following resources can be useful:

- The book *7 Kinds of Smart: Identifying and Developing Your Multiple Intelligences* by Thomas Armstrong is a good place to start.
  - This book includes assessments that can be answered in session, either individually or in groups, to help identify learning styles.
  - The book also includes "2 new kinds of smart" to total nine learning styles in all.
  - These learning styles are based on the concepts of multiple intelligence that were first explored by the psychologist Howard Gardner.
- Another resource is my own book, *The Joy Compass*, which devotes an entire chapter to matching mindfulness and contemplative practices with the various learning styles.

Here is a list of the nine intelligences, or learning styles:

1. Verbal-Linguistic
2. Visual-Spatial

3. Musical-Sound

4. Bodily-Kinesthetic-Tactile

5. Mathematical-Science-Logical

6. Social-Interpersonal

7. Reflective-Intrapersonal

8. Natural World

9. Existential-Meaning

CONCLUSIONS

Integrating learning styles is also a powerful way of tapping into someone's brain and how they most easily increase neural connections. One easy way to quickly grasp learning styles is to note what activities or hobbies an individual enjoys or has a passion for. That's something that can easily be accomplished during the initial intake session.

Remember, too, that by asking someone to practice mindfulness, you are asking them to learn new ways of making associations—with their thoughts, emotions, and the outside world. Consider using a learning style assessment like the one mentioned above in *7 Kinds of Smart* if clients have problems staying with a mindfulness practice.

Tip #4
Integrating Brain Science

THOUGHTS FOR THERAPISTS

Perhaps one of the most empowering messages of 21st century neuroscience is that our very thoughts and where we place our attention change the physical structure of the brain. The idea that it would be possible to change the brain *from the inside out* was thought to be fantasy only a few years ago. Most importantly, the significance of self-directed neuroplasticity (a term coined by psychiatrist Jeffrey Schwartz) is that it offers hope for anyone who feels stuck. Basically, self-directed neuroplasticity means that the power to change old behaviors and rewire the brain is possible through focused intention and attention.

As Pema Chodron writes in *Uncomfortable with Uncertainty*, "You might be the most depressed person in the world, the most addicted person in the world, the most jealous person in the world. You might think that there are no others on the planet who hate themselves as much as you do. All of that is a good place to start. Just where you are-- that's the place to start." But how is this kind of profound change possible?

The work of obsessive-compulsive disorder (OCD) specialist Jeffrey Schwartz has shown that a four-part mindfulness method can rewire around the faulty OCD circuit in the brain. Naturally, this capability for rewiring the brain has been shown to be effective for conditions such as depressive thoughts, rumination, anxiety, and pain.

A ROCKY METAPHOR FOR HOW THE BRAIN WIRES AND REWIRES

A useful metaphor for neuroplasticity that can be shared with clients is that of a rock-strewn hill. (This can easily be drawn on a whiteboard to illustrate for visual learners). Imagine a craggy hill that is filled with grass, rocks, and uneven surfaces. Now, visualize what it would be like to push a large rock all the way down to the bottom of this hill. It would take a lot of effort to push it over or around existing rocks and mashing down the long grass that is in the way. Now, suppose I continue pushing more rocks down the same pathway over and over and over again. What would happen? Most clients get the picture and rightly respond that *a groove, a rut*, or *a path* would form. Once that rut is in place, it takes almost no energy to push the next rock down the hill. Just set it into the groove and it rolls right down. This is how habits are formed.

Next, suppose I want to push the rock down the hill in a new direction. In other words, I want to create a change of habit! But this fresh area of the hill is rocky and grassy, and it takes a lot of effort to push the rock down to the bottom. Even after I've achieved this, the old rut still remains. It doesn't instantly disappear. So, that's the challenge of *re-wiring* the brain. Even as we make progress, the old rut is still there. Fortunately, if we keep pushing the "rock," or new behavior, down the hill over and over, a new groove or path will eventually form. Over time, if the old rut is not used, it will get covered over with new grass and obstructions. Now, we'll be using the new path, but it takes patience and persistence to develop it. This rocky metaphor actually describes how neuroplasticity works so the brain can wire and then re-wire itself.

TIPS FOR WORKING WITH CLIENTS

- Discussing neuroplasticity with clients makes sense. It gives them a view inside the brain and helps them learn that they can change behaviors through intention, attention, and repetition.

- Introduce clients to the practice of intention and attention—as will be discussed in more detail in the next chapter, Tip #5 – *Strengthening Intention and Attention*.

- Another related chapter that you may want to review is Tool #11, *The Power of Breath*. This intervention explores how stress affects the brain and how to engage the body's relaxation system.

Tip #5
Strengthening Intention and Attention

THOUGHTS FOR THERAPISTS

In their book *You Are Not Your Brain*, authors Jeffrey Schwartz and Rebecca Gladding write, "Helping individuals increase intentional and willful thought alters the brain's physical wiring and pathways . . ." In terms of brain science, intention makes us *pay attention* to our intention and the goals surrounding it. This process is what alters and rewires brain circuitry—which then changes how we will behave in the future.

To use a driving metaphor, intention acts as the steering wheel in the car that points us in the direction we want to go. Intention keeps our attention on the road, so to speak, instead of distractedly drifting off onto the shoulder, or worse. While our past history, trauma, and experiences may push us from *behind*, intention places us in the driver's seat, puts us in charge, and *pulls us forward*—to wherever we would like to go.

By working with clients to set intentions, you help them more strongly connect—or in some cases reconnect—to whatever is most important in their lives. This brings conscious focus to how they want to live and what is most important to them, including such things as health, emotional well-being, parenting, relationships, and career development. Intentionality is helpful because it can be applied to any domain or dimension of living.

It's worth noting that intentions do not always have to represent the *big picture*. Even the smallest of actions, from taking a step to chewing the next bite, can be done with intentionality—and thus, a heightened sense of purpose and awareness.

Intention-setting, whether for things big or small, is empowering for three important reasons. Firstly, it allows clients to direct their own path and decide how they want to address difficult areas in their lives. Secondly, it includes the concept of free will, which means that, as thinking beings, each of us is capable of transcending past habits, conditioning, unhealthy coping mechanisms, and addictive behaviors. Thirdly, intentionality brings attentional awareness to the conditions and situations the client is facing right now. This is critical, of course, because one must first become aware in order to change any behavior.

INTENTIONS ARE DISTINCT FROM GOALS

There is often confusion about the difference between goal setting and intentions, or intentionality. Intention as we are using it here is like a master plan or mission statement that sets out broad ideas and talks about values. To return to our driving metaphor, an intention is about your big picture desire to drive safely, respectfully sharing the road with others, and to be patient and aware when behind the wheel. Notice that this intention does not include any specifics about *how* to accomplish the intention.

In contrast, goal-setting is *how* you express your intention to change your behavior and thinking. In the case of driving a car, it would involve a specific action plan when going from point A to point B. For example, this might include such things as staying within the speed limit, knowing in advance your driving route and where to turn, courteously allowing space between your car and others, letting others merge into your lane, and reducing dangerous distractions by not texting while driving. This kind of goal-setting, or action plan can easily be tracked to see if one's behaviors are congruent or incongruent with an intention. If incongruent, then this can lead to more discussion—either a revision of the intention statement or better strategies and preparation for implementing the action plan and focusing attention on it.

TIPS FOR WORKING WITH CLIENTS

- Goals are often determined early on in the treatment planning process, but they do not always include an intention statement. This handout accomplishes that.
  - Use the exercise below to help clients develop a clear and purposeful "mission statement" for various big picture parts of their life that relate to the issues they face.
- A mindfulness practice, or tool, that works well with the *Creating a Personal Intention Statement* handout in this chapter is Tool #32, *The 'We' Cure*.

HANDOUT: CREATING A PERSONAL INTENTION STATEMENT

Instructions: Use this 3-step handout to write down a short statement related to an area in your life that you would like to improve or enhance. Have you ever done this before? If not, welcome to the club. Very few people consciously think about what values matter most to them and how this could change their lives. The nice thing about setting an intention (or personal mission statement) is that it is uniquely yours.

Below are several different life areas (with examples) of statements. A mission statement need only be a single paragraph (about 3-4 sentences long). As you begin, here are some guidelines:

1) Your mission statement does not have to be perfect! In fact, part of this assignment is that you go back over and over to rewrite and rework it. Personal statements take time to craft, so be patient with yourself and know that you will, more than likely, change it in the future.

2) Your mission statement *will not include specific goals.* This is a broader statement that relates to the values you want to bring to any area of your life. The goals come later.

3) Think about sharing your statement with those who you trust. Find out if others have statements like these. Or, you can examine the intentionality of someone you admire—this could be a historical figure, a friend, or a family member.

Step 1.   Choose from one of the following LIFE AREAS for your Personal Intention Statement:

- Physical Health
- Emotional Health

> **Example:** *My intention is to find balance each day so as to nurture my mental health. I will make time to notice and value the little things that are already at my side. Also, I will open myself to positive resources and others as a way of finding hope and resilience.*

- Parenting
- Marriage/Relationship

> **Example:** *My intention is to create loving relationships that manifest the values of respect, cooperation, kindness, generosity, harmony, and ease. I commit myself to bringing patience, honesty, and transparency into the relationship.*

- Friendship
- Financial
- Daily Joy
- Career

> **Example:** *My intention is to bring an attitude of deep appreciation and gratitude to my work. I will strive to have my work serve others in a helpful and supportive way.*

Step 2. Use the *values list* below to identify the values that matter to you. **Circle** those *value* words that matter to you and which feel right to include in your statement:

- trust
- patience
- respect
- forbearance
- generosity
- hospitality
- transparency
- attentive
- supportive
- acceptance
- self-acceptance
- curiosity
- empathy
- relational
- humility
- compromising
- friendliness
- loyalty

- appreciation
- gratitude
- patience
- peace
- kindness
- harmony
- hopefulness
- service
- nurturing
- altruism
- sensitivity
- prayerfulness
- faithfulness
- expressive
- grateful
- sharing
- willingness
- persistence

- openness
- caring
- compassion
- honesty
- humor
- cooperation
- joyfulness
- calmness
- understanding
- benevolence
- spirituality
- encouraging
- thoughtfulness
- gracious
- judicious/fair
- love
- tenderness
- reliability

If you have additional words or phrases not noted above, write these here:

_____

_____

_____.

Step 3. Using the value words you chose, write a first draft below:

My Personal Intention Statement for (Family, Career, etc). _____ is as follows:

_____

_____

_____

_____

_____

_____

_____

_____

Reflections:

1) How does it feel to have a personal intention statement? What is one way your commitment to this statement could create a positive difference for you or others?

_____

_____

_____

_____

_____

_____

_____

2) What specific goals or actions can you think of that would support your intention? Write these down below. Make sure these are small and simple goals to begin with! You can track your goals to make sure that you are supporting your intention to the best of your ability.

_____

_____

_____

_____

_____

_____

_____

_____

_____

3) Consider carrying your statement with you by writing it on an index card and looking at it several times daily. How can you develop a plan to accomplish this?

_____

_____

_____

_____

_____

_____

_____

_____

Tip #6
Working with the Anxious Client

THOUGHTS FOR THERAPISTS

Clinical anxiety is the most frequently diagnosed mental health condition in the United States. There are some 40 million Americans who struggle with an anxiety disorder. This is not so surprising considering that there is also an epidemic of 21st century stress that people confront because a variety of circumstances, including technology overload, work and deadline pressure, and a faster and faster pace of life.

The cumulative effect of these and other stress factors are akin to walking on a tightrope, always fearful of falling and never really being able to let down one's defenses. Often, those individuals who experience anxiety may be living in their heads and are disconnected or dissociated from the body. For this reason alone, getting a client to breathe and get present in the body can be somewhat scary for him or her.

How can you help an anxious client overcome their resistance to the any of the body or breathing-oriented practices in *The Mindfulness Toolbox*? Below are some tips for working with such clients.

TIPS FOR WORKING WITH ANXIOUS CLIENTS

- Help anxious clients to understand that they are probably already breathing shallowly—which has the effect of making them more vulnerable to the body's alert and alarm system.
- Many anxious individuals hyper-focus on bodily sensations. They may, for example, impose a catastrophic thought onto a body sensation: *My heart is beating rapidly or my hands are sweating so that means I'm having a heart attack!*
  - In these cases, let them know that the purpose of a breathing or body practice is to help them learn the difference between an actual *sensation* in the body and the *thought* about that body sensation.
- Normalize the client's anxiety, letting them know that it is okay to initially get more anxious when first learning this practice. Reassure the client that over time this practice will become easier.
  - Remind the client that much anxiety comes from trying to avoid or resist anxiety in the first place. The first step towards getting less anxious is to not resist the experience of it.
- By encouraging anxious individuals to become more familiar with the body, they will eventually grow more at ease with the whole range of sensations that are part of a human body.

- *The Mindfulness Toolbox* contains a variety of body-sensing practices that can assist in helping with this process of getting to know the body. Look these over to see which might be most appropriate for a particular clients needs:
  - Tool #12, *Palming the Present Moment*
  - Tool #13, *Ground-Surfing (Mindful Walking)*
  - Tool #16, *BE-THIS Sense Grounding*
  - Tool #17, *Sensing and Rating the Body*
  - Tool #33, *Squeeze Out Stress*
  - Tool #41, *Surf the Body (The Body Scan)*

- Finally, it's important to accept that being human means feeling anxiety from time to time! This is part of the human experience. Although we don't want to feel anxious all the time, neither is it realistic to think that we should *never* experience anxiety.
  - Anxiety can serve as an important and useful signal from the body telling us that something in our life needs to change.

Tip #7
Working with the Depressed Client

THOUGHTS FOR THERAPISTS

Several new studies have explored how a mindful breathing practice can help with symptoms of depression. For example, research published in *Cognitive Therapy and Research Journal* in 2011, demonstrated how paying attention to the breath actually helps to reduce rumination, negative thoughts, and depression. The study also reported how subjects demonstrated reduced fearfulness when noticing sensations in the body. Findings such as these are important since depressed clients often focus on, and often get stuck in, negative thinking patterns.

On the contrary, focusing on the breath helps by turning attention away from those negative thoughts and onto the breath. The ability to shift focus and broaden our attention is vital for overcoming rigid and ruminative thinking. Fortunately, this kind of mental adaptability and flexibility is a skill that can be learned, even when wrestling with depression. Below are a few ideas for applying mindfulness to depressed clients.

TIPS FOR WORKING WITH DEPRESSED CLIENTS

- When applying any of the *Mindfulness Toolbox* practices, one good idea is to get clients started in *small*, *realistic*, and *achievable* ways. This might mean, for instance, that a practice could be performed just one minute a day to begin. What's important is that clients find success, even if it comes in small increments.
- Have clients schedule their mindfulness practices or activities in advance—ideally, right during the session. If they don't have a scheduler, they can get one and bring it into the session.
  - It's also a good practice to inquire, "What obstacles might make it difficult for you to do this practice?" Another idea is to have the client create a back-up plan in case the initial practice time is missed.
- Ask clients to check in with a follow-up call, e-mail, or other method of contact after completing their task. This is a good way to bring some accountability and a shared relationship to the practices.
- In addition, enlist clients in those mindfulness tools and practices that best match their preexisting learning style. A mindful movement or mindful walking practice, for example, will be more effective for someone who finds it difficult to sit still. Discovering a client's favorite activity or hobby can be a good place to start.
  - Refer to *Tip #3 – Tapping into a Client's Learning Style*.
- Consider utilizing a mental rehearsal or visualization technique as a way to help depressed clients to become more energetic, overcome isolation and engage with others, or let go of stress. Since motivation has been shown to begin *after* someone

starts doing any activity—be it exercise, overcoming procrastination, or engaging in a pleasant activity—even two minutes of a mental rehearsal will serve as a good motivator.

- There are several mental rehearsal activities and ideas in *The Mindfulness Toolbox*. For more information on these, check out the following chapters:
  - Tool #18, *Visualizing the Calm*
  - Tool #30, *Activating with Mental Rehearsal*
  - Tool #37, *Warm Hands Visualization*
  - Tool #39, *Be the Pebble*

• Finally, work with the client's story and personal metaphor to help the client find a new, more enlightening and empowering view. The brain responds to language and symbols; metaphor is an effective way of activating the brain and connecting with how your client views the world.

- For handouts that address facilitating change through the power of language, meaning, and metaphor, refer to the following:
  - Tip #1, *Expanding Your Mindfulness Vocabulary*
  - Tip #9, *Working with Children and Adolescents*
  - Tool #20, *Overcoming Perfectionism*
  - Tool #24, *Change Your (History) Channel*
  - Tool #38, *Share an Uplifting and Hopeful Story*
  - Tool #45, *Decentralizing Pain*
  - Tool #46, *Reaching Beyond the Cocoon of Pain*

Tip #8
Working with Stress and Burnout

THOUGHTS FOR THERAPISTS

Stress occurs when the biological and psychological reactions to anxiety, fear, overload, and chaos in life and the environment exceed one's ability to cope with it. In *Undoing Perpetual Stress*, author and psychotherapist Richard O'Connor explores how our ancient brain and nervous system are not designed to adequately manage modern stress. With eight of every ten commonly used medications prescribed for symptoms of stress, O'Connor further states: "Contemporary research shows that you can't fully recover from any of these [stress-related] conditions by focusing on the symptoms. You have to change the way you live."

The Mindfulness Toolbox is designed to address the bio-psycho-social model by reducing the negative effects of chronic stress that suppresses the immune system and creates disease and imbalance. It is no wonder that millions of people deal with stress-related illness. Fortunately, mindfulness techniques promote change from the inside out by increasing awareness of a client's negative habits and behaviors. Awareness is the first step to making positive change and going off auto-pilot.

Burnout, on the other hand, is produced by the combination of a culture of overwork, accelerated work and life pace, self-abusive overwork behavior, porous work-home boundaries, and unrealistic demands that destroy joy, hope and meaning. Job stress has been shown to produce a lot of unhealthy behaviors, from excessive eating to bringing work stress behavior home.

Stress and burnout sap joy from life, while the journey to revitalizing oneself can be satisfying and meaningful. Note that even the behavioral ideas and strategies below integrate well with mindfulness in the sense that they encourage greater awareness, collaboration, motivation, and constant practice to bear fruit.

TIPS FOR WORKING WITH STRESS AND BURNOUT

- Pay attention to how much sleep a client is getting. Sleep is a buffer against stress, and even just two to three days of not enough sleep can trigger a chronic stress state in the body by producing too much cortisol.
- Mindful self-care is a wonderful antidote for stress, and there are several tools and strategies for doing this in *The Mindfulness Toolbox*. To be effective, self-care needs to help clients achieve the following:
  - Get proper nutrition, especially protein throughout the day.
  - Avoid meal skipping and being aware of hunger cues.
  - Limit excess caffeine, especially if it may be affecting sleep.
  - Exercise or walk for 30 minutes a day or longer.

- Develop a supportive social network.
- Create healthy boundaries with technology, especially before sleep.
- Develop a mindfulness practice for countering stress.

- One proven way to reduce stress is to notice where it's coming from and to simply avoid it. This might include making a daily stress record and seeing what things might be altered—such as taking a route to work that circumvents that stress-inducing rush hour traffic jam.

- Burnout can be helped by following the stress tips above, in addition to helping clients accomplish the following:
  - Find a story of hope and rebirth from the client's history.
  - Share or discuss a story of hope with trusted others.
  - Locate resources that speak to the idea of rebuilding and starting anew.
  - Start a gratitude practice that refocuses attention in a positive way.
  - Transition from work to home in a healthy way that discharges negative feelings and allows for a secure reattachment to loved ones.
  - Rediscover and reconnect to what brings feelings of passion and joy in life.

EASY WAY TO ASSESS STRESS

There is an easy-to-use 10-question stress instrument called the *Perceived Stress Scale* (PSS) that was developed by psychologist Sheldon Cohen at Carnegie Mellon University. The test measures stress levels by examining such things as negative affect, life events, and perceived stress that individuals report having experienced over the past month.

The assessment only takes about 10 minutes to complete and score, and there are even versions of the PSS available online. This is a useful tool for starting a dialogue about stress with clients. By the way, caregivers tend to score in the "high" range with the PSS. (So you may want to check this out for yourself).

Tip #9
Working with Children and Adolescents

THOUGHTS FOR THERAPISTS

Bringing mindfulness concepts to children and adolescents can present some unique challenges. This group, which has been referred to as *digital natives*, is more connected to technology than perhaps any group in history. A national study released by the Kaiser Family Foundation— "Generation M2: Media in the Lives of 8- to 18-Year-Olds"—found that the amount of time spent using media by this impressionable group had increased dramatically. The time that they spend watching media of all kinds equals more than 53 hours per week, or almost 7 ½ hours a day!

This study dovetails with other recent studies that examine how multitasking negatively affects the ability to focus concentrate and study. Consider, too, that increased technology use can impact one's ability to sleep—which is a necessary component for learning. Studies in the field of interpersonal neurobiology (IPNB) have also shown that live, face-to-face interactions at a young age are critical for wiring up the brain's prefrontal cortex—that part of the brain that helps create secure attachment, the ability to have empathy, and to develop attuned relationships.

Taken as a whole, the impact of technology overuse may be producing a perfect storm for children and adolescents as far as learning and the development of the social brain are concerned. Fortunately, mindfulness can act to counterbalance some of these influences.

TIPS FOR WORKING WITH CHILDREN AND ADOLESCENTS

- Include a "technology usage assessment" with your initial intake. Typically, this needs to include the following items:
  - Amount of time spent daily using technology (at school and at home).
  - How technology is used prior to going to sleep.
  - How technology is used during periods of study.
  - Weekly and yearly usage of video games.
  - Amount of usage of Facebook and other social media sites.
- Make mindfulness skills fun and engaging.
- Use technology metaphors (unplug, reset, reboot, etc.).
- Find mindfulness "apps" that can help clients pay attention to such things as sleep deficits (yes, there's an app for that!), breathing, and coming back to the present moment.
- Support ways of replacing technology with Nature breaks and social activities with friends and family.

Tip #10
Working with Pain

THOUGHTS FOR THERAPISTS

Chronic pain is a condition that many clients face. Pain of any kind can dramatically affect mood, relationships, and the ability to function on a daily basis. Unfortunately, doctors may feel they have no other option but to prescribe powerful painkillers. Many clients and patients, however, object to the cognitive and other side effects of these medications. With mindfulness, you can present clients with an option for managing pain that may help them to reduce the level of pain meds they take—and in the process help them to find a new way to experience pain.

It was in the late 1970s that Jon Kabat-Zinn adapted early Buddhist mindfulness practices to help patients deal with chronic back and muscular pain. One component of mindfulness-based stress reduction that he utilized was to help patients notice sensations in the body moment by moment. The practice, called "the body scan," allows for patients to change their relationship to the sensation of pain.

This is not to say that mindfulness can replace medications. Mindfulness is like a useful supplement, a portable practice that can refocus attention in new ways to give patients in pain some more control over their situation.

TIPS FOR WORKING WITH PAIN

Working with pain will let you choose from among numerous mindfulness approaches. The interventions and handouts in Section 5, *Mindfulness Tools for Pain*, bring together a diverse set of options, including:

- Visualization and guided imagery.
  - Tool #43, *The Bear Meditation*
  - Tool #50, *At Peace with Pain*
- Narrative storytelling and metaphors that help reframe pain and create a meaningful story around the pain.
  - Tool #42, *Attitude of Acceptance*
  - Tool #45, *Decentralizing Pain*
  - Tool #46, *Reaching Beyond the Cocoon of Pain*
- Refocusing attention in new ways that reduce psychological distress and perceived intensity of pain.
  - Tool #41, *Surf the Body (The Body Scan)*
  - Tool #44, *Focusing Away*
  - Tool #49, *Healing with Music*

- Self-compassion and loving-kindness practices to help one get through the process.
    - Tool #47, *Lessons from Nature*
    - Tool #48, *Loving-Kindness Affirmation*

CONCLUSIONS

As with all the mindfulness practices in *The Mindfulness Toolbox*, understanding the patient's learning style will go a long way toward helping the client find a way to inhabit a body that is in pain. Working with the emotions of anger, frustration, grief, loss, and disappointment requires a special compassion and empathy on the part of the therapist. Helping clients use mindfulness to invite patience and self-compassion for the losses and suffering that the journey of pain brings can open new doorways of understanding and hope.

Section 2

MINDFULNESS TOOLS FOR ANXIETY

Tool #11
The Power of Breath

THOUGHTS FOR THERAPISTS

As I once wrote in *One-Minute Mindfulness*, "Your breath is your intimate kiss with this moment." In truth, it is much, much more than that. First, it is a fundamental means by which we can biologically regulate the mind and body and calm the reactive core of the brain. In fact, it's so effective that it is a central means of teaching arousal control to training Navy Seals. Second, diaphragmatic breathing is effective with anxiety and depression because it refocuses the attention away from unproductive mind wandering, as well as anxious thoughts about the future.

By practicing diaphragmatic breathing, also known as belly breathing, we are reconnecting with that same natural, effortless form of breathing that we enjoyed as a baby and young child. But over time, in response to stress, the longer, deeper belly breath became more and more shallow. And the shallow, rapid breath in the upper part of the lungs is exactly what makes us more vulnerable to the body's fight and flight stress response. Fortunately, we can relearn our original default breathing method. It's kind of like reinstalling your body's original programming and rebooting your mental equipment so that it all runs optimally.

Best of all, the idea of taking a calming breath to center oneself is found in cultures around the world, and I have yet to find a culture that doesn't appreciate the idea of breathing as a way to calm down. To introduce the idea of breath, I always like to find out if a client has ever been taught diaphragmatic breathing, and whether they use it and have found it helpful.

TIPS FOR WORKING WITH ADULTS

- Don't assume that a client understands how to do belly breathing properly—even if they state that they have already learned it. If someone is using the wrong technique, they may not be getting the full benefits of this practice.
  - Have the client demonstrate how she or he belly breathes. This lets you know whether or not the client is doing this correctly.
- It is helpful to describe how breathing turns on the body's built-in relaxation system. This scientific perspective helps patients grasp how the breath actually engages the thinking part of the brain and blocks reactivity and unhealthy emotions.
- If you are dealing with an anxious client, refer to Tip #6, *Working with an Anxious Client*.

TIPS FOR WORKING WITH CHILDREN

Children tend to be quite adept at learning the power of self-soothing through this practice. This practice is useful for all the family members to use in order to calm down.

- When teaching belly breathing to children, you will want to adapt the teaching as described in the handout.
- It is often helpful to get children to blow bubbles. Ask them to blow a bigger bubble, and they will need to exhale a longer and slower breath—which is a belly breath. (In contrast, a short, punctuated breath will produce many tiny bubbles).
- Another idea is to have children to blow on a pinwheel and keep it spinning for as long as they can—again requiring a long, slow breath.
- Instruct children to lie down and place a balloon or piece of paper on their belly. Then, ask them to move the object just by breathing. (Belly breathing is easier when lying down on the back or the side).

A QUICK BIOLOGY LESSON ABOUT THE VAGUS (NOT THE LAS VEGAS) NERVE

Basically, diaphragmatic breathing activates our relaxation system—or what I like to call the air conditioning system of the brain and body. Simply put, diaphragmatic breathing keeps the reactive core of the brain from overheating. Here's how breath accomplishes that in three easy steps:

1. A belly breath causes the lungs to press on the diaphragmatic wall.
2. The diaphragmatic wall in turn pushes down on the abdominal cavity. (Think of balloon that's being squeezed.)
3. The squeezed abdomen spreads outward in the front of the abdomen and the back where it presses on the spine. This causes the abdominal cavity to put pressure on the longest cranial nerve—*the vagus nerve*—which runs all the way down from the brain stem and the spine. When pressed on, the vagus nerve quiets down and turns on the body's relaxation system and regulates the parasympathetic nervous system. (This is in stark contrast to what I affectionately call the "Las Vegas nerve" of the body—the instant gratification nerve.)

THE RELAXATION SYSTEM

You may not want to give clients the entire scenario, but it's a pretty cool and elegant system that we carry with us at all times. Here's the quick rundown of what happens when the vagus nerve gets quieted down:

1. Lowers blood pressure, pulse rate and respiration
2. Cleanses lactate from the blood (lactate increases feelings of anxiety)
3. Increases alpha brain waves (calm and alert)
4. Releases the neurotransmitter serotonin (95% of this feel-good neurotransmitter is stored in the stomach lining and intestines). Serotonin gets into the bloodstream and up to the brain in about 20-30 seconds

Voilà! No wonder breathing helps you feel better and think more clearly.

RESEARCH ON THE BRAIN AND BREATHING

Research has shown that just twenty minutes of diaphragmatic breathing is all that's needed to activate and oxygenate the mindful and thinking part of the brain (the prefrontal cortex).

Suffice it to say, you can share as much or as little of this information as you want. Personally, I find that many adults enjoy learning and talking about the science of breathing—which by the way, activates the thinking part of the brain.

Use the following handout to guide clients through the breath practice.

HANDOUT: LEARNING TO BELLY BREATHE

Instructions: Have you ever seen a baby breathe? With each breath its little belly moves, not the chest. That's our natural breathing method, and with this handout you will learn to use belly breathing, or diaphragmatic breathing, to naturally relax the body.

If you're a chest breather, you're taking shorter, faster breaths. By getting the air in the deeper part of the lungs, you'll actually get 10x more air with each breath. This will be a slower, longer breath—but a *normal* sized breath. **Follow along with the questions below to retrain the breath and get the benefits of belly breathing.**

Question 1: Am I a Chest Breather or a Belly Breather?

To check whether you are breathing shallowly or more deeply, do the following:

1. Sit in a chair, with an erect but comfortable posture.
2. Place one palm on your chest and the other palm on your stomach (below the rib cage and above the navel).
3. Take some normal breaths. Which hand or hands move? If you're not sure, look in the mirror.
4. If the top or both hands are moving, then you're a chest breather. If the bottom hand moves, you're getting a fuller breath. In either case, follow along to get the most out of your belly breathing.

Question 2: How Can I Retrain Myself to Belly Breathe?

You are going to learn a movement that gently stretches muscles that run between the ribs—naturally hinging the ribs open so you can get a more full breath.

1. Reach behind your chair with your arms and bring your hands together.
2. Relax the abdominal muscles so your stomach can move outward as your lungs press on the stomach cavity.
3. Notice if there's more movement in the belly. It's that easy.
4. If you didn't notice any belly breathing, try this posture: raise your arms above your head and clasp your hands behind your neck. This opens the chest area and makes taking a deeper breath easier.

Question 3: How Should I Practice or Use Belly Breathing?

1. Try practicing for 1-minute at a time, three times a day to start.
2. You can notice when you feel tense or stressed, and do a minute right then.
3. Pay attention to your posture, especially if you're sitting at a computer.
4. Practice while standing up or lying down.

Reflections: What time(s) of the day can you practice breathing? _____

_____

_____

_____

Are there any challenges you see to using belly breathing? _____

_____

_____

_____

How would this breathing benefit you? _____

_____

_____

_____

Tool #12
Palm the Present Moment

THOUGHTS FOR THERAPISTS

Anxious clients are often caught up in a myriad of thoughts spinning in their heads. For some, this rapid spinning of thoughts can even result in an overpowering sensation of nausea—almost like being on a boat that is bouncing up and down in choppy water. That makes sense when you consider that it has been estimated that the mind can generate up to 125 thoughts per second. Getting solidly rooted or grounded back in the body is one method for calming down, quieting the anxious or ruminating mind, and getting back onto more firm and peaceful ground.

In addition to anxiety, this practice is a good way of creating space from any negative emotions, anxious or ruminative thoughts, and feelings of being overwhelmed from stress or chaos. I also recommend this as a tool for when clients come into the counseling office and are not settled down due to the demands of time pressures, traffic congestion, getting a parking space, etc. Spending a minute or two getting grounded and centered at the start of a session can help the client enter a more receptive space.

One of the advantages of the *Palm the Present Moment* practice is that is portable and easy to use. It offers a multi-purpose means of centering to counter anxiety—especially when transitioning from one physical location or situation to another. (This is also a useful one-minute mindfulness technique for therapists to use between sessions for the same reasons.)

TIPS FOR WORKING WITH CLIENTS

- *Palm the Present Moment* practice is a readable script that you can use in session to guide clients through the practice. Do this prior to giving them the handout.
- Follow along with the movements so patients can visually see you model this practice for them.
- Other sense grounding practices for anxious clients that can be bundled with this one include:
  - Tool #13, *Ground Surfing*
  - Tool #16, *BE-THIS Sense Grounding*
  - Tool #33, *Squeeze Out Stress*
  - Tool #35, *Take a Stress Pause*

HANDOUT: PALM THE PRESENT MOMENT

Instructions: Use this portable grounding meditation script whenever you find yourself getting anxious, worried, feeling overwhelmed, lost in negative thoughts, or feeling uncertain about the future while transitioning from one place to another. Spend as much time as necessary to do this the first time.

Once you are familiar with how to *Palm the Present Moment*, you can shorten the process and do this in just one-minute, if desired.

Sit in a comfortable chair and take a couple of nice, long, calming breaths. Now, just raise your hands up to the height of the heart center, with the palms facing one another—about a foot or so apart. Notice how much tension there is in just holding the arms and hands up in the air.

Next, ever so slowly, bring the hands closer until you feel even the slightest or subtle sensation of energy, pressure, heat, or warmth. Stop when you feel this, and just notice this for a few moments. Observe closely this sensation. Is the heat, warmth, energy, or pressure constant? Or, does it vary slightly moment to moment?

Now, gently move the palms closer until just the fingertips come together with the most feathery, lightest touch. Imagine that the molecules from the fingertips of your right hand are dancing with the molecules of the fingertips of your left hand. You might even think about what dance they are doing . . . the foxtrot, the samba, the tango, the waltz, or the jitterbug.

Now, you continue to bring your palms together until they lightly touch. As you do this, notice how the fingers straighten out and how more heat builds up between the palms. With your palms together, this is a good time to pause for a few moments and have appreciation for the body, which is a precious gift that we possess.

We can also reflect on the words of former priest and author John O'Donohue who wisely wrote in Anam Cara: A Book of Celtic Wisdom, *"Your body is the only home in the universe."*

(Rest in silent appreciation for 5-10 seconds)

Now, let's spend a few moments to see what it's like to tense, and then relax the body. Keeping your palms touching, raise your elbows up to the side. Press with only ten percent of the total pressure you could exert. Now, press your hands together even harder—up to twenty percent of total pressure.

Stop pressing if you feel any pain. Press only as hard as you can without experiencing pain or discomfort.

Again, observe how far up your arm the tension goes. Does it extend to the wrists, the elbows, the shoulders, the shoulder blades, the back, the chest? Maybe you feel more heat building in the palms of your hands? Which muscles are tense? After about five seconds of this, let your shoulders and elbows relax and fall. Release all this tension. Notice how nice it is to let go of tightness and tension in the body.

Finally, very slowly open your palms, like flower blossoms opening to the morning sun. Sense the coolness in your palms as the heat dissipates. Finally, let the weight of gravity tug on your hands and arms, letting these gently fall like leaves from a tree, until they come to rest on your lap or legs. Take a nice, long inhale, and as you exhale, imagine all the remaining stress draining out with the exhale down your legs and out of the bottom of your feet—where it will flow into the Earth for recycling.

If you want, just sit for a few more moments in appreciation for the body that follows your commands and carries your consciousness so you can achieve your life goals. How marvelous!

Tool #13
Ground-Surfing (Mindful Walking)

LEARNING STYLES

Depending on how mindful walking is practiced, it can be suitable for a surprsingly wide range of learning styles. This makes it highly adaptable to a large number of patients.

While movement is naturally visual-spatial, bodily-kinesthetic, and reflective-interpersonal, there are other learning styles that can be tapped into simply by incorporating the adaptations mentioned below, in italics.

Verbal-Linguistic—*Instruct clients to make walking an intention-setting practice, which involves the stating of an intention prior to making the next movement, such as "taking a step," "turning," "lifting the foot," etc.*

Visual-Spatial

Musical-Sound—*Instruct clients to notice all sounds--from the sound of their foot touching down and the subtle sound of the breath to all other sounds in the environment.*

Bodily-Kinesthetic-Tactile

Social-Interpersonal—*If clients enjoy walking with others, have them be aware of movement, shared communication, or even silence during the walk.*

Reflective-Intrapersonal

Natural World—*Have Nature-centered individuals pay special attention to Nature's wonders while walking, including taking time to pause and observe Nature's diverse colors and sounds.*

THOUGHTS FOR THERAPISTS

Human beings are historically an itinerant species. As hunter-gatherers, we moved in order to survive. Even today, movement is as natural to us as breathing. For many, however, movement also brings anxiety, because movement often occurs during moments of transition, such as driving in the car to get somewhere or walking into a staff meeting. When you think about it, transition often brings uncertainty—because we're not sure what our transition will bring. It is thus no surprise to find that anxiety naturally peaks around or during times of transition.

Transition can highly impact relationships. If, for example, someone has difficulty transitioning from work to home, the ability to relate to loved ones at home will be impaired. It's not unusual for individuals to carry around workplace stress long after they have left the office. This is why practices such as mindful walking or movement offer a more effective way of consciously transitioning.

Keep in mind that there are many ways to get fully embodied with movement, from a practice of yoga and qigong to mindful walking, so see if any of these might be of interest to patients.

It's also worth noting that movement with awareness is especially useful for those clients who may have ADD or who struggle with anxiety during periods of transition. Bringing focus to one's movement can very powerfully shift someone away from anxious thoughts or from worrying about what is to come. Instead, it helps them to calm by focusing them into their present-moment experience.

TIPS FOR WORKING WITH CLIENTS

- Mindful walking is ideal as a method for reducing anxiety during transitions. Check out the following chapters for other helpful, present-moment grounding techniques:
  - Tool #12, *Palming the Present Moment*
  - Tool #16, *BE-THIS Sense Grounding*
  - Tool #23, *Here and Now Pleasantness*
  - Tool #31, *The Lightness of Laughter*
  - Tool #35, *Take a Stress Pause*

It may also be useful to consider asking one or more of the following questions when thinking about how and when to best apply a mindful movement practice:

- What transition moments are most difficult for you each day (driving in traffic, returning home, etc.)?
- How does anxiety affect you when returning home after work?
- What do you do in the car while driving from work to home?
- How do you usually reconnect with your family when returning from work?
- How much time do you spend between arriving home and entering the home environment?
- If there were one thing you would like to change in your behavior related to coming and going from home, what would it be?

HANDOUT: GROUND-SURFING (MINDFUL WALKING)

Instructions: Use this portable method of getting present when you are in transition and feeling anxious as you walk from one place to another. Consider using this practice when walking from the car to your office, walking from the car to entering your home, or even when walking into that staff meeting.

To begin with, 1) find a place that is quiet, where you can take up to fifteen steps in any direction, and 2) practice next to a wall just in case you lose your balance since you will be moving more slowly than normal.

You can do this practice in two ways. Try each of the methods below for three minutes and see which one works best for you:

Ground-Surfing with Intention:

As you prepare to walk, set an intention for each step and movement you take. This can be a mental intention, said silently. For example, you can set the intention to "take a step with my right foot," after which you will follow up by taking that step. As you take the step you will observe and notice very closely how it feels as your foot lifts up, moves forward, touches down, and even how it feels as you shift the weight from one side of the body to the other. In other words, this is really a simple three-step process of 1) setting an intention, 2) following up with an action, and 3) noticing and observing the movement in detail. It's that easy!

Usually, you can set an intention for each step, and also set an intention for every time that you turn the body in a new direction. That mental intention can be stated just as "turning, turning."

Spend three minutes walking down a hallway or corridor in your home or office, then turning and walking back. Setting an intention will naturally slow you down. It will also tend to keep your mind from thinking other thoughts. If, however, your mind has thoughts or gets distracted, simply return to stating your intention for each step and return to the walking. Try this in the morning as a way to walk to the bathroom, or during other times of the day.

Note that you can use intention while walking at normal speed as well! In this case, simply state the word "walking, walking" as you move, placing full awareness on the legs, the feet, the arms, and the entire body as it moves.

Ground-Surfing with Full Presence:

For this practice, you don't need to think of anything or set any mental intention. Instead, you will imagine placing your full awareness in the body itself. It is as if your consciousness moves into your legs and feet, and you can notice each little movement and be fully engaged with it—just as if you were a surfer riding a wave in Hawaii! Only this time you're surfing the ground, noticing every little change in how your feet contact the carpet, wood, or grass that you walk on. See how each surface affects how you surf it.

Let your body and movement become fluid and enjoy the ride as you immerse yourself in this dance of movement. Have you ever seen someone practice tai chi, yoga, or dance? Let walking slowly (or even at normal speed) embody the same graceful movement as these practices. By moving in this way you take the body off auto-pilot and flow with each movement and moment. Enjoy the ride!

Reflections: Which of the two ground-surfing methods above helped you to stay fully present with each movement? Which slowed down the busy, anxious mind?

_____

_____

_____

When would be a good time for you to practice ground-surfing? How could you adapt this practice to help manage anxiety during periods of uncertainty and transition?

_____

_____

_____

How could you create a daily mindful movement practice? What would that look like? What challenges or obstacles would you face in implementing this?

_____

_____

_____

Tool #14
Two Ways of Doing Chores (Or, How to Savor the Moment)

THOUGHTS FOR THERAPISTS

There are a lot of ways to change habits and to get someone off auto-pilot. One method is to get them experiencing even the ordinary in a new and fresh way. Look at what two seminal thinkers of the last century had to say about noticing the world around us.

> *Boredom is simply lack of attention.*
>
> —Fritz Perls, the founder of Gestalt Therapy

> *There are two ways to live your life:*
> *one is as though nothing is a miracle,*
> *the other is as though everything is a miracle.*
>
> —Albert Einstein

Historically, our wisdom traditions have used rituals to radically shift awareness. Rituals often take activities considered ordinary and mundane—reading, sharing the family meal, or drinking tea—and transform them into an experience of the extraordinary. Some examples of this are sacred reading, or *Lectio Divina*, in the Christian tradition, the family Sabbath ritual in the Jewish tradition, and even the secular tea ceremony as practiced in Japan. But is it possible to accomplish this shift even while doing the laundry, washing the dishes, or other humdrum, daily chores?

There's also the question: *What does such a shift of awareness accomplish?* What this really does is to demonstrate the difference between an *outcome orientation* and a *process orientation*. Why is an outcome orientation problematic? An outcome orientation is focused on the future, which often produces worry or anxiety about achieving a desired outcome. In a very real way, it saps the enjoyment and curiosity out of the experience itself.

Learning how to change focus from outcome to present-moment process can be a powerful experience. Most importantly, it reduces anxiety that comes from focusing on expectations and outcome-oriented thinking.

Here are a few examples of an outcome orientation:

- Learning for the sake of getting that 'A' on a test or report card
- Finishing a work task on time
- Focusing solely on a sports training goal or time
- Getting that promotion at work
- Receiving the highest review from a supervisor
- Making sure the house is always spotless
- Comparing one's progress against that of others

By shifting awareness to the *most minute and tiniest details of one's experience*, the process orientation comes into the foreground. This practice also trains the brain to stay in the moment. The benefits of taking an attitude of curiosity and openness can teach anyone a new way to experience—and relish—any activity in which they are engaged.

TIPS FOR WORKING WITH CLIENTS

It's important to let clients know that focusing on the present doesn't mean that having goals is without merit. It doesn't mean that one will become a slacker! By all means have goals; the point is that *only* focusing on the outcome can be counterproductive and limiting. It only lets someone see one part of the picture.

It might also be helpful to ask clients how they have experienced goals in the past:

- Was there a time that you really, really enjoyed something just for the sake of doing it?
  - What was that event or situation? How did it feel not to worry about the outcome?
- When was the last time you accomplished a large goal?
  - Did it feel overwhelming?
  - What attitude did you have as you approached that large goal?
  - Did you do a little bit at a time? Or did you try to do it all at once?
  - What do you think it would be like to savor almost any activity?
- Here are some related chapters that focus on shifting awareness toward the moment. These can work in conjunction with *Two Ways to Do Chores*, as a way to give the client more experiences of powerfully contacting the here and now:
  - Tool #11, *The Power of Breath*
  - Tool #16, *BE-THIS Sense Grounding*
  - Tool #22, *The G.L.A.D. Technique*
  - Tool #23, *Here and Now Pleasantness*
  - Tool #34, *Turning Down the Volume with Nature*
  - Tool #35, *Take a Stress Pause*

HANDOUT: TWO WAYS OF DOING ANYTHING
(OR, HOW TO SAVOR THE JOURNEY)

Introduction: Have you ever thought that there could be two ways of doing anything? For example, you can wash the dishes to get them done with because they're a chore you don't like . . . or, you can do the dishes in order to do the dishes.

Likewise, you can drive your car to get from point A to point B . . . or, you can drive your car in order to drive your car.

Here's another example. You can do your homework or office work in order to get the best grade, highest accolades, or get a promotion . . . or, you can do your work with a sense of curiosity, openness, and total engagement.

In any of the cases above, you still get to your intended goal—of washing the dishes, driving where you want to go, and getting a positive response to your work. What's more, you savor the journey. That means you are less likely to feel pressured, anxious, or unhappy about the activity before you, or to have an unfortunate accident along the way because you were wishing you were somewhere else!

Even Henry David Thoreau experienced the problem of being present when he was living and walking around Walden Pond in the mid 1880s—and he didn't have an iPhone or iPad to distract him! Here's what he wrote in his Essay on Walking:

> *It sometimes happens that I cannot easily shake off the village. The thought of some work will run in my head, and I am not where my body is; I am out of my senses . . . What business have I in the woods if I am thinking of something out of the woods?*

Instructions: *Choose from among one of the following activities. It might be useful to choose an activity that you typically resist or don't like doing.*

Driving	Homework	Preparing meals
Washing the dishes	Laundry work	Shopping
Vacuuming	Studying for a test	General cleaning

The point of this practice is not to say you will suddenly love washing the dishes and will run over to your neighbor's house and volunteer to wash the dishes stacked in their sink! The idea is to change your relationship to an activity. To experience it in a whole new way that lets go of your previous assumptions and dislikes.

Do the activity for five or 10 minutes without distraction or multi-tasking—so turn off the TV or other devices and see what it is like to focus, slow down and notice every little detail that you can. Allow yourself to experience this chore or activity as if it were the very first time you have ever done it. Using the example of washing dishes:

- *Before starting, spend a few moments just to reflect on the dishes and utensils and how they have helped you enjoy your meal. Take a moment to admire the work and craftsmanship that went into designing and making these items.*
- *Feel the fine movements of your arms, hands, and body as you lift and manipulate the dishes.*
  - *Notice the coolness or warmth of the water as it splashes on your hands.*
  - *Sense the weight, texture, and shape of utensils and plates*
- *Notice the smells and scents of the dishwashing liquid.*

- *Observe all the unique colors and shapes on the dishes as if you had never seen them before.*
- *Listen to the sound of the water and the clinking of plates and cups, and other sounds in the environment.*
- *If you get distracted, return to the sensing of each moment.*

Reflections: What did you notice most by slowing down and immersing yourself in washing the dishes (or other activity)?

_____

_____

_____

_____.

What daily activities do you typically avoid or rush through? How would a more curious attitude change your experience of that activity?

_____

_____

_____

_____.

How could the idea of "two ways of doing anything" become a daily practice? In what way would it be helpful to you? How would it be helpful to those around you?

_____

_____

_____

_____.

Tool #15
Sky Gazing with Nature

THOUGHTS FOR THERAPISTS

There are many ways to find a balanced perspective during times of anxiety or emotional distress. Balance or clarity can be found cognitively, through soothing words or a more realistic understanding of events. Balance can also be sought non-verbally, through seeking out Nature. The brain, in fact, is highly attuned to Nature, and research by psychologist Stephan Kaplan at the University of Michigan has led to an understanding of how Nature works to restore depleted mental energy and increase focus. His work sparked interest in the field of what is known as *Attention Restoration Theory*.

Of course, at another level, Nature can provide us with the benefit of wise insights, as well as an abiding sense of peace and calm. Whether someone is mentally exhausted, fatigued from overwork or constant problem-solving, the *Sky Gazing with Nature* practice here acts as a means of getting grounded and centered. Best of all, it only takes a few minutes.

TIPS FOR WORKING WITH CLIENTS

- This practice is easily adapted to anyone's work or daily schedule. *Sky Gazing with Nature* can be done during a break while at work, in the morning, or in the evening.
  - Consider teaching this practice along with Tool #47, *Lessons from Nature*—a calming practice that demonstrates how to look at Nature in a fresh, insightful, and meaningful way.
- It is also useful as a transitional practice, much like the mindful walking practice.
- It is especially helpful if the patient or client has had a strong connection to Nature in the past.

HANDOUT: SKY GAZING WITH NATURE

Instructions: *Sky Gazing is a method of connecting your gaze with Nature. It begins by extending the gaze toward the sky or horizon, and then slowly bringing it downward to focus on a nearby tree or a plant.*

This short, easy-to-use practice can be done indoors or outdoors in a matter of minutes. Use it any time you are feeling mentally fatigued or anxious about an upcoming event. Whether you are a businessperson, student, teacher, or anyone overwhelmed by stress, this practice will help you get centered, refreshed, and quiet the busy mind. After you are done, you will likely feel more refreshed, and ready to focus and concentrate.

While you can use this practice indoors by using any size plant, the ideal method of practice would be out of doors with a large tree and a view to the sky or horizon. Follow along with the 5-steps below for approximately five minutes:

1) First, go outside and find a location that allows you to tilt your head up slightly so you can view the sky. Secondly, find a large tree that is situated near your view of the sky—so that you can easily transition your gaze from the sky to the tree while standing in place. In addition, you will want to be standing within arm's length of this tree. If that is not possible, stand close enough to see the details of the bark and leaves of the particular tree. When choosing a tree, make sure you pick one that is pleasing to you and draws you in. Perhaps it's the color of the leaves, the shape of the branches or the trunk.

2) To begin, slowly raise your head and cast your gaze out as far as you can into the sky. Visualize releasing and letting go of whatever troubles and worries you have into the expansiveness above you. Let go of the uncertainty, the not-knowing, the fear, the sadness, the doubt, and even the wishing-it-were different. Release all of that into the sky, which is infinitely spacious and big enough to hold all the worries of the world. Stand as long as you need to, continuing to let go and let be.

3) Place your hands on the tree as you shift your gaze from the sky down to where you connect with the tree. Imagine that your feet are rooted solidly into the earth like that tree. Did you know that trees are the largest organisms on earth? Feel your connection with the great cathedral of trees that protects our ecosystem and makes our lives possible. As you feel the bark on your hands and fingers, let yourself get absorbed into the big picture of how we are surrounded and sustained by the natural world.

4) Now, starting at the bottom of the tree, slowly turn your gaze upward. Pay attention to the smallest details, from the texture of the bark and changes in coloration to where new growth occurs. Continue to broaden your focus until your gaze reaches the highest branches at the top of the tree.

5) Rest the weary mind as you sense your unity with Nature and the wisdom it holds. Appreciate that the natural world has lessons to offer on how there is a season for planting, growing, and harvesting, and pausing. Allow yourself to open to these teachings in the moments or days ahead.

Reflections: What was it like to spend five minutes with Nature in this way? When might you find this practice most helpful?

_____

_____

_____

_____

_____

What was it like to release and cast your worries into the expansiveness of the sky? Did this help you gain a different perspective?

_____

_____

_____

_____

_____

Tool #16
BE-THIS Sense-Grounding

LEARNING STYLES

The following learning styles are compatible with this practice:

Visual-Spatial

Musical-Sound

Bodily-Kinesthetic-Tactile

THOUGHTS FOR THERAPISTS

Sense-grounding—getting connected to any of the senses through hearing, sight, smell, taste and touch—is an evidence-based practice for constructively distancing from anxious thoughts, rumination, craving, and emotional negativity. Grounding practices have even been shown to be helpful when someone is experiencing trauma, flashbacks, PTSD, or other extremely high levels of negativity.

Grounding practices are not meant as replacements for other long-term methods of dealing with trauma or flashbacks. Yet they are important because they serve as an invaluable, effective, and portable means of helping patients self-regulate at times of negative triggering. The ability to practice grounding almost anywhere can be especially helpful when other resources may not be available.

For anxious clients or patients who are often "in their heads," the *BE-THIS Sense- Grounding* is an ideal, multi-purpose method for engaging all the senses and coming back to the present moment. The practice also builds up a patient's confidence in his or her ability to de-escalate from negativity and be more in control.

TIPS FOR WORKING WITH CLIENTS

The handout below integrates different forms of mindful sense-grounding. The *BE-THIS Sense Grounding Practice* utilizes all the five senses.

- As a prelude to the *BE-THIS Sense-Grounding Practice*, start with Tool #11, *The Power of Breath*. This will familiarize the client or patient with the diaphragmatic breathing, or belly breathing practice that is built into *BE-THIS Sense-Grounding*.

- You may want to couple this practice with the demonstration of a second grounding method:
  - Tool #23, *Here and Now Pleasantness*—offers a form of mental and visual grounding that is predominantly based on pleasant images, objects, and even memories.

It may be helpful to follow along with the steps below when working with clients:

1. Have clients rate themselves on a 1-7 scale *before* you guide them through each of the practices—with 1 as the lowest level of emotional reactivity and 7 the highest.

2. Read the handout as a script to guide the client through an in-session demonstration of *BE-THIS Sense-Grounding*. (Optionally, as mentioned above, you can also teach Tool #23, *Here and Now Pleasantness*).

3. Immediately after experiencing the grounding methods, have the client or patient re-rate her or his level of emotional reactivity or negativity on the 1-7 scale.

4. Problem-solve with the client to determine which of the mindful grounding methods was most effective.

5. Give handouts of the grounding methods to patients to take home as practice guides.

CLIENT PREPARATION FOR USING BE-THIS-SENSE GROUNDING

Advise clients to prepare for grounding by doing the following:

- Always practice grounding *before* trying to use it in a real world situation. Mindful sense-grounding is a skill, and skills take time to learn. Try practicing for at least 10 minutes a day, or longer, for up to a week.

- Carry your grounding handout with you, or record it and carry the recording with you. Follow along if necessary when using your preferred grounding method.

- If possible, do your grounding where you won't be interrupted or distracted.

- Ground yourself as long as needed to get calm or centered.

HANDOUT: BE-THIS SENSE-GROUNDING PRACTICE

Instructions:

WHAT: "BE-THIS" is an acronym that stands for six powerful grounding skills (Breath, Emotion, Touch, Hearing, Intentional Stretching, Sight/Smell) that put you in touch with all your senses. This lets you redirect your attention away from anxious or negative thoughts and focus on your surroundings in a more positive way.

WHEN: Use "BE-THIS" when you notice emotional overload, such as when you might rate your negative or anxious state as being in the "5-7" range, or high range, when rated on a scale of 1-7, where 1 is the lowest negativity and 7 is the highest.

HOW: The four steps to practicing the "long form" BE-THIS are as follows:

Step 1. Notice when you have gone into emotional overload, which you can do by rating your level of negativity. You don't have to wait until you reach the "high" range to do grounding. In fact, it is a good idea to start practicing early on, when you notice that your level of negativity is in the medium 4-5 range.

In the space below, write down the clues that let you know when you are in the 5-7 range of emotional overload. In other words, what does your emotional overload look or feel like? (For example, this could be a feeling you have in your body, wanting to cry, a sense of anger or helplessness, etc.) The trick is to notice this before you overreact emotionally, or during your emotional overload.

_____

_____

_____

_____

_____

_____

Step 2. Look around and describe your surrounding environment in a single sentence, followed by your intention to practice BE-THIS awareness skills. This could be stated as, "I am standing in the living room at home, and I am practicing my awareness and grounding skills." The purpose of this is to center you in the moment. Practice this right now by writing a sample intentional statement below:

_____

_____

_____

_____

_____

Step 3. Find a place where you can spend approximately five to seven minutes to practice in peace. This can still be done with others present, but it is best when distractions are limited.

Step 4. You will cycle yourself through the BE-THIS sense awareness and grounding skills. You can spend approximately one to one-and- a half minutes with each of the BE-THIS grounding skills. Right now, practice each of the six grounding skills as described below:

**B—Breathe**. For the first minute, use the diaphragmatic breathing practice to stay grounded in breathing. As you move on to the other senses, continue to keep about 25% of your awareness on your breathing.

How did it feel to do this first part of the exercise?

_____

_____

_____

**E—Emotion**. For the next one to one-and-a-half minutes, let yourself experience your emotions and feelings with a sense of acceptance, without either pushing them away or attaching to them. Just name or label your emotions as if from a safe distance—without adding any judgment of good or bad, by simply saying "feeling of anger" or "feeling of sadness". You might even say where you feel this in your body, such as "tightness in my stomach" or "clenching in the jaw." As you continue to do this, notice if the feelings are less intense or change.

Practice by naming your present emotions/body feelings in the space below. If you're not exactly sure what name to give the emotion, take your best guess and write it down anyway. In this way you are getting to know your feelings a little more closely.

_____

_____

_____

If someone else is involved in your emotional overload, spend another 30 seconds or one minute to notice if it is possible for you to experience empathy with regards to this person. Empathy means imagining how another person feels. It doesn't mean they are right and you are wrong, or vice versa. It just means that you could understand how they might be feeling. If you don't feel empathy, just notice that you don't feel this. When the minute is up, move on.

What thoughts came up for you while doing this portion of the exercise?

_____

_____

_____

**T—Touch**. For one minute you will practice relaxing touch. Raise your hands to heart level, with your palms facing one another and a few inches apart. Sense any heat and pay attention to your pulse until you can feel it in your hands. Then, take three breaths, each one filling the space between your palms with positive energy. Then, slowly bring your palms together, compressing the energy. Briskly rub your palms together for a few seconds.

Next, place your hands over your eyes for a few moments, then one hand over each temple, then over the back of your head. Let the energy in your hands relax and soothe you. Next, you can place your palms over the top of your chest and slowly sweep them downward over your heart, stomach, thighs, and knees. Lastly, let your arms hang at your side and shake your hands for a few seconds to release any remaining tension.

What thoughts came up for you while doing this portion of the exercise?

_____

_____

_____

H—Hear.   For one minute, tune into the sounds of your environment. Let yourself expand your hearing and awareness to let in as many sounds as are possible—even those you make by breathing, moving in your chair, etc. Try listening to each without putting a name or label on it. Just notice each sound, occurring moment-to-moment, second-to-second.

Again, write down whatever thoughts came up for you while doing this portion of the exercise.

_____

_____

_____

I—Intentional Stretching.   For the next minute, set a simple intention and follow up mindfully. You might set the intention to stretch your neck by rolling your head around from right to left in a relaxing circular movement. Or, you might set the intention to raise your arms high over your head as you inhale, then lowering them as you exhale. It's a good idea to think of an intention that helps you release some tension and tightness from the boy.

In the space below, write down some gentle body movements (such as those mentioned above or others) that you could use as an intention and which would help you to relax.

_____

_____

_____

S—Sight/Smell.   For the final minute or longer, use your olfactory, taste and visual senses with curiosity. Do this without thinking about the function of an object, or whether you like or want or dislike it. Simply look around and notice *in detail* as many different shapes, sizes, and colors of objects as you can—noticing these with an attitude of openness, child-like wonder, and interest. Also, what different scents are in the environment?

Look around the room or environment you are in at this moment. After you have spent time exploring, take a moment to note in the space below some of your observations about the sights and scents around you:

_____

_____

_____

Wrap-Up: Congratulations on completing the *BE-THIS Sense-Grounding* practice!

Now that you have completed the practice, go ahead and re-rate your level of emotional negativity on a 1-7 scale. How has the number changed?

If grounding has been helpful, write down examples of times when this practice could have been helpful in the past, as well as how you could use it in the future. Remember that *BE-THIS Sense-Grounding* is like any skill. The more you practice and use it the better you get at it!

_____

_____

_____

OPTIONAL PRACTICE: *Speed Scan BE-THIS-Grounding*

Sometimes you don't have five or six minutes to reverse overload! Fortunately, you can scan through all of the BE-THIS Sense Grounding skills in just a minute or less.

As before, you can rate and then re-rate your level of emotional negativity on that 1-7 scale both before and after you do the *Speed Scan BE-THIS Grounding*.

Set the intention to do *Speed Scan BE-THIS*. Then, simply state each letter and the word that it represents. Then, you will follow it with a brief experience as follows:

B-Breath: take one or two deep and satisfying diaphragmatic breaths.

E-Emotion: Quickly scan your body from head to toe, sensing for an emotion or feeling in the body. Name that feeling.

T- Touch: Slowly touch one thing nearby or press your feet into the ground.

H-Hear: Notice a single sound that is happening at this very second—even if it is the sound of your breath.

I-Intentional Stretching: State a simple intention to do a single stretch, and follow it up right now.

S-Sight and Smell: Notice one object in front of you, and take one long inhale to see what scent you can detect in the environment.

Tool #17
Sensing and Rating Anxiety in the Body

THOUGHTS FOR THERAPISTS

With forty million Americans facing anxiety on a daily basis, anxiety disorders are the most prevalent of all mental health issues. Patients often hyper-focus on sensations in the body and then impose catastrophic thoughts onto those sensations. Many anxious patients would prefer to stay "up in the head" and not get into the body. Unfortunately, trying to avoid the body only creates more resistance and exacerbates fear and anxiety. The mindfulness approach here is designed to help individuals become friends with the body as they slowly learn to inhabit and embody it.

Patients struggling with anxiety often cannot distinguish between the sensation and the thought. The anxious thought becomes thoroughly woven with the sensation, like a single fabric. Through this observation process used here, patients will discover that the sensations in the body are just sensations. Thoughts about the body—even catastrophic ones—are very different from sensations. Further, patients will learn firsthand how the body's sensations are always changing, dynamic, and transitory.

A second benefit of this body awareness practice is that body signals and sensations become objects of awareness. This is like taking a step back to notice what is happening, rather than seeing it and experiencing it through one's own eyes. This is an effective and safe means of self-distancing from any anxious, frightening, or scary feeling in the body. It's important to note that it is not disassociating from the body. Rather, it is an intentional and conscious means of stepping back in order to carefully observe the body.

In addition, labeling a sensation in the body has another important function. Labeling or naming feelings in the body engages the brain's frontal cortex. The frontal cortex then sends inhibiting signals back to that part the brain (the amygdala) that triggers the fight, flight, or freeze response.

TIPS FOR WORKING WITH CLIENTS

When helping anxious clients get into the body, it may be useful to:

- Start slowly. You may want to get clients warmed up with the following centering body practice:
  - Tool #12, *Palming the Present Moment*

- Normalize this process by letting clients know that befriending the body takes time. Developing patience is an important aspect of this practice.

- The more frequently that one practices naming and rating sensations, the more benefit that will be derived from it. Practicing even when *not* feeling anxiety can be useful.

- Identify the cause of anxiety. Some anxiety, for example, is produced not from past trauma or conditioning, but because of daily work and life stress. The body is an effective early warning system for signals of stress. Recognizing these signals is important, and clients can best respond by noticing and honoring the signals, as well as finding ways of reducing, managing, or preventing daily stress.

- To increase clients' commitment to this or other mindful practices, ask if they believe they are worth "three minutes" a day of taking care of themselves in this way. Refer to Tip#2, *Making Mindfulness Effective* for more information about using *The 3-Minute Question* for clients.

HANDOUT: SENSING AND RATING ANXIETY IN THE BODY

Instructions:

For this exercise you will learn how to pay attention to sensations of anxiety that occur in the body in a whole new way. This is a portable practice that can go with you anytime you feel anxious. It is also a useful way to "drop into the body" anytime throughout the day—just to say "hello" and get more familiar with this precious gift that we all possess!

There is no better early warning system than the body for signaling us we may be out of balance with some situation—either past or present—in our life. Whether the body's signal is related to old trauma, a difficult life situation, or stress, the ability to notice these warning signals can help you respond more quickly and effectively.

Remember, no one is immune from anxiety! By *Sensing and Rating Anxiety in the Body* you can be present with it and cope with it in a healthy way. The practice of noticing sensations takes time, so be kind to yourself as you learn how to do this. If possible, do this practice in a quiet location so you can observe the sensations in detail.

Follow along with the six steps below:

1) Begin this practice when you first notice any sensation of anxiety. If you wait until a full-blown anxiety attack is underway, then it could be difficult to even practice this technique! The more you do this practice, the more easily you will begin to notice the early onset of anxiety—whether it's just a tightness in the chest or a shallower than normal breath.

2) Bring your palms together and press your heels into the floor as a way to get grounded in the body. Press them together for about 5 seconds, then exhaling to let go of stress.

3) Bring attention to where you are feeling anxiety in the body and answer the questions that follow.

   If you are alone, you can either state the answers out loud or write them down in the space provided. (If you are with others while experiencing anxiety, simply state the answers mentally).

   a. *Where in the body is the sensation of anxiety present?* Name as many different places as you can, from where there's the strongest feeling to the smallest feeling.

   _____

   b. *How would you rate the anxiety level on a 1-7 scale, with 1 the lowest level of anxiety and 7 the highest level?* Write that number below.

   _____

   c. *If the anxiety sensation had a name, what name would you give it?*

   _____

   d. *If the anxiety sensation had a color, what color would it be?*

   _____

   e. *If the anxiety sensation had a shape, what shape would it be?*

   _____

   f. *If the anxiety sensation had a size, how large or small would it be?*

   _____

g. *If the anxiety sensation had a weight, how heavy would it be?*

_____

4) For one minute, take several slow, calming and soothing breaths. As you do this, you can visualize or imagine that this breath travels into the place where you are experiencing the sensation of anxiety. Let the breath fill up that area. With each exhale, you can visualize the sensation draining out of the body.

Optionally, instead of focusing on breathing, you can simply observe the sensation with as much curiosity as you can! Like a surfer riding a wave, see if you can surf the anxious sensation, noticing in great detail every little change as it rises and falls—just like an ocean wave.

5) At the end of one minute, go back to Step 3 and re-rate the level of the sensation on a 1-7 scale, as well as answering the questions about name, size, shape, color, weight, etc.

6) Continue to observe the sensation for up to five minutes, noticing how it changes moment by moment, even subtly.

Reflections: What did you learn from noticing and rating your sensation of anxiety?

_____

_____

_____

_____

When can you routinely schedule the *Sensing and Rating the Body Practice* as a way of noticing the early warning signs of anxiety?

_____

_____

_____

_____

Tool #18
Visualizing the Calm

THOUGHTS FOR THERAPISTS

The practice of visualization, or mental rehearsal, has long been used to help everyone from professional athletes to Navy Seals improve performance. The advantage of a mindful mental rehearsal for therapy is that it is portable and can be practiced almost anywhere. What is more, it has been shown to help rewire the brain from the inside out. Suppose, for example, that someone visualizes being interviewed for a job in advance of the upcoming interview. That means that when they go in for the actual interview, it's really the second time they've done it.

Naturally, that first experience—even though it is a mental one—will help prepare an individual for how to act or respond to the "actual" situation. Research studies comparing mental rehearsal with actual practice have shown that similar brain activity occurs in both cases. A mental rehearsal can be adapted for many different situations. It can help activate or create energy in someone who may be isolating, or it can be used to produce a state of calm and lessened anxiety in those who find certain situations to be triggering.

TIPS FOR WORKING WITH CLIENTS

- Combine this practice with diaphragmatic breathing, Tool #11, *The Power of Breath*, which is useful for arousal control and calming the emotional core of the brain.
- Practice visualization with great attention to engaging all the senses, including sight, hearing, touch, smell, etc.
- Make sure clients successfully complete the activity imagined in their mental rehearsal.

HANDOUT: VISUALIZING THE CALM

Visualizing the Calm (Situational)

Instructions:

For this exercise you will learn how to use the power of visualization, or mental rehearsal, to find a greater sense of calm when faced with a situation that is distressing or anxiety producing. Mental visualization, for example, has been shown to be effective with athletes because it helps them actually practice, as well as prepare for dealing with the high stress level of competition.

This practice works because the brain responds as if it is actually experiencing the visualization. What is important, however, is that you engage all your senses in your mental imagery. Picture your calming scenario in as much detail as possible. That means noticing all the sights, sounds, smells, textures, and any other sensations that surround you. Like in the film *Avatar*, where the main character was linked to an *avatar* that was controlled through his mind, you can think of this visualization as your own 3-D avatar!

Pre-Visualization:

1) Identify the activity during which you feel anxiety. Write that in the space here:

_____

_____

_____

_____

2) Next, identify when you first start to experience any sensation of anxiety. What is that sensation? Write that here:

_____

_____

_____

_____

3) Now, identify the following: What are you typically doing prior to the start of your anxious feeling? What are you thinking? What are you feeling?

_____

_____

_____

_____

Visualization:

For your visualization, picture yourself at the point *before* you notice any sensation of anxiety. See yourself as totally relaxed, calm, and at ease—even knowing that you are going to be encountering a situation that has *in the past* produced feelings of anxiety.

Now, picture yourself, or your *avatar*, entering that situation while continuing to be totally at ease and relaxed. Notice all the people, the objects in the room, the sounds and sights all around you. You may even notice the particular scents that are in the space. It is important that you mentally see yourself as being successful at being calm and at ease in your visualization.

If at any time you feel tense or anxious, remind yourself that this is *your* visualization! You can always freeze-frame the action, put the visualization into reverse and back up to the point where you again feel secure and calm. Then, start rehearsing, or playing, your visualization again. Stay connected to your soothing breath as you play through the rehearsal.

After you complete your rehearsal, practice again . . . and again! You can always imagine yourself as more and more confident and relaxed, which lets you be more flexible and helps you prepare for any unpredictable events that might happen while you are in "real" time.

Reflections: Congratulations on completing this mental rehearsal! How did it feel to successfully complete it?

_____

_____

_____

_____

Think of one small way that mental rehearsal can make a difference for yourself or others. How could you practice this each day for up to five minutes? Where and when could you practice?

_____

_____

_____

_____

3-Minute Visualizing the Calm Right Now

Here is a second visualization practice, and it is for those times you need to calm down and counter general feelings of anxiety and chaos in the moment, before it overwhelms you. For this visualization, you will draw upon your personal history.

Is there something or someone from your past that has helped you to find peace or calm? This could be any object, sound, color, or even a caring family member or friend. Even if this resource is not available at the time of your anxiety, you can draw upon your memory to rehearse a detailed visualization that brings relief.

For the next three minutes, visualize of one or more of the following favorite, reassuring, and uplifting items in as much detail as you can.

Favorite color(s)	Favorite wise person	Favorite healthy food
Favorite song or sound	Favorite peaceful place	Favorite animal
Favorite natural setting	Favorite quote	Favorite soothing activity

Tool #19
Get Free from the Monkey Trap

LEARNING STYLES

The following learning styles are compatible with this practice:

Verbal-Linguistic

Reflective-Intrapersonal

Existential-Meaning

THOUGHTS FOR THERAPISTS

A few metaphors that signify anxiety in the body include such phrases as *being all clenched up*, *tight-fisted*, and *having our insides tied up in knots*. The question is: How can we help clients who are *wound up tight* to let go and loosen their grip on things as they are? Even a little bit? This is not an easy task, but the following handout offers a tactile and visual meditation for letting go. It also demonstrates just how easy it is for us to be stuck and attached to that thing that might be causing untold pain and suffering! In fact, we may have a very good reason for not wanting to let go.

The story and meditation in the following handout is one I first used in my book *The Mindfulness Code*. In the original context, the story and meditation were about letting go of craving. But in the bigger picture, it is really about letting go of anything that we are strongly, or in some cases, obsessively attached to.

It is based on a story I once read of how hunters used a particular method for capturing monkeys. I'm not sure if the method here is apocryphal or not, but one thing is for certain—it is an effective example and metaphor for how we can get all clenched up and frozen in place. What is more, it demonstrates how effortlessly we can get free from suffering simply by letting go. Of course, it's never really so simple or easy.

TIPS FOR WORKING WITH CLIENTS

- Before using the meditation in the handout, have clients explore and reflect more deeply on what monkey traps exist in their lives, and what it would be like to let themselves out of these.
  - Monkey traps can take the form of a rigid belief system, such as feelings of inadequacy, and worthlessness, etc. that drive the client to experience anxiety.
  - Monkey traps can also be an unrealistic thinking style, such as "should" thinking, catastrophic thinking, perfectionism, and personalizing, etc.

- When working with perfectionistic thinking, consider combining this practice with Tool #20, *Overcoming Perfectionism.*

- This story and meditation are a starting point, not a final solution.

- Letting go of old habits and anxiety can be frustrating and scary. These are natural reactions.

- Practice, practice, practice because letting go of anxiety is a skill.

HANDOUT: STORY AND MEDITATION: HOW TO GET FREE FROM A MONKEY TRAP

Did you know that hunters have a unique way of capturing monkeys? They hollow out a gourd or container and place some food inside. The gourd is fixed to the ground, and there is a hole barely large enough for the monkey's hand to fit through and grab the tempting morsel.

However, there's a catch . . . and that is that the once the monkey grasps the food with a clenched fist, its hand is too big to pull out. Yes, the monkey *could* get unstuck by releasing the food and yanking out its hand. However, the iron grip of attachment, greed, and desire for this food keeps the hand clenched. The monkey is trapped by nothing more than his own unwillingness to let go.

This is a powerful metaphor for our own "stuckness," or anytime we are trapped by a strongly held belief, rigid idea, or desire that keeps us frozen in place. In addition to feeling stuck, we may likely experience feelings of helplessness and hopelessness. Fortunately, you can learn what a monkey caught in a trap does *not* know: *The secret to getting free from almost any anxiety producing trap or unbending belief system is simply learning to let go of it.*

Get Free from the Monkey Trap Meditation

Instructions:

Before reading through the meditation, begin by answering the following questions to help you discover those "monkey traps" in your own life.

Pre-Meditation Questions: Everyone deals with some kind of monkey trap in their life. The trick is to first become aware of the trap (which the monkey couldn't do) in order to get free. What are the traps that cause your anxiety or tension?

Keep in mind that any idea or strong belief—such as the need to get all "A's" in school, to always be first in any endeavor, or to fear messing up and not being liked—can create anxiety. And yet, you find it difficult to stop believing that you must achieve or act in a certain way—even if it causes immense pain. Write down your "traps" below, even if you still think they are necessary for you.

_____

_____

_____

Ask yourself, "How strongly does this idea or belief hold onto me, onto my mind, and my emotions? You can even rate this on a 1-7 scale, with 1 being no hold on you, and 7 representing a "super glue" hold on you. Also, rate this in the space below.

_____

_____

_____

_____

Monkey Trap Meditation: Now, you are ready for the Monkey Trap Meditation. Find a place that is quiet calm. Sit in a chair, taking an erect but relaxed posture.

> *Visualize your 'monkey trap' or the cause of that anxiety or dis-ease and dis-comfort as being located in that gourd that traps monkeys. Now, imagine extending your arm and squeezing your hand through the gourd's narrow hole and grabbing on to whatever it is that you feel is absolutely necessary to have. Notice how this is actually a form of grabbing onto, attachment, and craving.*

As you hold on, focus on how tightly your hand is clenching on to your craving. Feel how tight and painful it is to hold on like this. Keep holding and feeling the sensation that comes from this kind of grabbing and holding on so tightly to something.

Now, ever so slightly, give yourself permission to let go of the craving, to let go of that idea or belief that you believed that you *must absolutely possess*. What would be so horribly bad about letting go of it? Would you be a pariah? Would you have no other options in life? Notice how the craving can be so narrow, limiting, and overpowering that it can make us forget about other possibilities! As you let go of the craving, or monkey trap that holds you, simultaneously release the tension in your hand.

Spend at least two minutes slowly letting yourself release and let go of this craving. You might say to yourself, "In this moment, I can relax my mind, relax my hand, and relax my need to grab onto the craving." Slowly release your clenched fist. Feel how the blood returns into your hand. Notice how your hand has freedom of movement. Observe the pleasant sensation that comes from letting go. Now, slowly extract your hand from the "monkey trap" and leave your craving behind for the moment. Shake your hand and fingers for a few seconds, savoring the freedom of full movement that they now enjoy.

Use this simple meditation each day, or whenever you need help you deal with feelings or beliefs that constrict you and keep you clenched up and tight with anxiety.

Reflections: How did it feel to let go in this way? To what extent did this mediation change the perception of your craving or lessen how strongly you are holding onto your "monkey trap"?

_____

_____

_____

_____

_____

_____

_____

Tool #20
Overcoming Perfectionism: The 70% Rule, or Why 7 is the New 10

THOUGHTS FOR THERAPISTS

The perfectionism trap is easy to fall into. After all, we live in a culture that is very much oriented toward success and achievement. Everything has a shadow side, however, and the shadow of perfectionism is false promise of controlling results and avoiding the pain that comes from experiencing disappointment, failure, loss, and rejection. While the idea of avoiding pain sounds reasonable, perhaps even laudable, there is no way to avoid loss in life, just as there is no way to maintain perfection. In *Present Perfect: A Mindfulness Approach to Letting Go of Perfectionism and the Need for Control*, psychologist and author Pavel Somov insightfully writes, "Perfectionism costs money, time, and resources. Perfectionists might be prone to fix what isn't quite broken, to redo entire projects because of minor perceived imperfections and flaws. While perfectionism offers the short-lived reassurance of structure from the ambiguity and uncertainty of life, ultimately it constrains your choices and sense of freedom. In sum, perfectionism is an existential trap."

Unfortunately, the effort invested in trying to be perfect and avoid loss or failure in life also comes at a great emotional cost—sowing the seeds of anxiety, fear of failure and loss of joy to a self-critical and unforgiving attitude toward oneself and others.

Accepting failure does not suggest that one can't strive for excellence. Rather, it makes the point that failure and loss are vital steps toward personal growth because that is how we learn. It is how we deal with life's unexpected curveballs that we learn resilience, perseverance, and optimism.

The handout below capitalizes on the strengths of not controlling the outcome, as well as the helpful lessons that come from failure.

TIPS FOR WORKING WITH CLIENTS

- Explore perfectionism in the client's family history.
- Help the client examine the advantages and disadvantages of perfectionist thinking and behavior.
- Use the handout to help further the client's understanding of perfectionism. Consider using this practice with the following:
  - Tool #19, *Get Free from the Monkey Trap*

HANDOUT: THE 70% RULE, OR WHY 7 IS THE NEW 10

Instructions:

This handout is a worksheet for learning about *The 70% Rule, or Why 7 Is the New 10*. Basically, this rule suggests that it's practically impossible to consistently reach 100%, or get a perfect "10" in any endeavor. You can try, but you will put in a lot of extra effort and sweat for very little return.

Think of it this way: Putting an additional 20-30% energy into what is already *very good* or *good enough* may not be a practical use of your time. To find out if this is really so, answer the questions in Part 1 of this worksheet to understand and consider the role of perfectionism in your life and whether it is counterproductive. The questions in Part 2 will examine whether the substitute goals of *very good* or *good enough* have merit.

PART 1:

Reflections: Do you delay starting a project because you know it must be perfect?

_____

_____

_____

Similarly, do you delay completing projects because you worry they won't be good enough?

_____

_____

_____

How worried are you about how others will judge your work? Are you your own worst critic—thinking you could have done better? Do you feel that any effort of less than 100% is a failure?

_____

_____

_____

Have others said you are highly critical of them? How has this attitude affected your relationships?

_____

_____

_____

Look over the reflections above to see if perfectionism is creating difficulty or havoc in your life or relationships. Now, continue with Part 2 of this worksheet.

PART 2:

Redefining Failure: In the space below, write down your own definition of failure. Does your definition include the importance of failure for what it teaches you about resilience, self-acceptance, and other kinds of learning? Consider including how failure or loss prepares you for later success.

_____

_____

_____

How would letting go of the craving for a perfect outcome remove self-imposed pressure? How does it lessen anxiety or worry?

_____

_____

_____

How could putting in 70% of your energy toward the goal of *very good* or *good enough* be helpful to you—especially since that other 20-30% can never make anything perfect anyway?!

_____

_____

_____

Right now, think back on an experience where you were overly critical or dissatisfied with your work or performance. Now, using the new definition above, reappraise and re-rate how well you did using a 1-10 scale, where a rating of 7 (*very good* or *good enough*) is really a 10.

_____

_____

_____

Section 3

MINDFULNESS TOOLS FOR DEPRESSION

Tool #21
Sharing Gratitude

Use this effective gratefulness intervention for mild to moderate depression as a way to turn attention toward feelings that are both sustainable and positive.

LEARNING STYLES

Gratitude is one of those rare practices that spans the entire range of learning styles. Because of this, gratitude can be experienced and adapted in ways that are compatible with all of the learning styles:

Verbal-Linguistic

Visual-Spatial

Musical-Sound

Bodily-Kinesthetic-Tactile

Mathematical-Science-Logical

Social-Interpersonal

Reflective-Intrapersonal

Natural World

Existential-Meaning

THOUGHTS FOR THERAPISTS

Gratitude is a means of shifting awareness and attention. It truly is a core mindfulness practice that can alter our mood—not to mention how we can perceive reality. Research has shown that gratitude is an evidence-based practice that is useful for mild to moderate depression. One study titled "Counting blessings versus burdens: An experimental investigation of gratitude and subjective well-being in daily life"—conducted by psychologists McCullough, Emmons, and Tsang and published in the *Journal of Personality and Social Psychology*—found that those subjects who focused on gratitude and kept a journal reported themselves as being happier, more optimistic about their lives, and even exercised an hour and a half more per week than those subjects who did not practice gratitude.

In her book, *Gratitude*, inspirational author Melody Beattie reminds us:

> *Look closely at the ordinary in your life. While you're being grateful, don't forget to express pure, sheer gratitude for how beautiful the ordinary really is. We can easily overlook the ordinary and*

take it for granted. The sun rises and sets, the seasons come and go, and we forget how beautiful and sensational the familiar really is.

There are many forms of expressing gratitude. There's the *basic gratitude* that Melody Beattie touches on in the aforementioned quote. This includes those commonplace and familiar things that are so easy to take for granted—like a roof over our head, a plentiful water supply, and a bed to sleep on, just to name a few.

Going a step further, there is *paradoxical gratitude* that applies to those things we'd rather not have in our lives, but could be thankful for just the same. Maybe we are addicted, but we could still be grateful for those support resources that can help us move us forward. No wonder that gratitude is a big part of 12-Step programs.

Working with clients on gratitude can be a fulfilling experience. It's just one more thing to be grateful for.

TIPS FOR WORKING WITH CLIENTS

- See if a patient's religious or spiritual background is compatible with a gratitude practice. All wisdom traditions stress the importance of gratitude.
- Find a way to make gratitude interpersonal, since it is an ideal way to build and strengthen relationships.
- Share the ideas of basic gratitude and paradoxical gratitude with patients, to see if they can find these in their own life.
- Gratitude alters more than mood state. It can affect how one experiences the body. Help clients to notice how gratitude makes them feel at the body level—perhaps even by giving them more energy.
- Let clients know they can start small. Even thinking of one gratitude per day or a week is good enough—remember Tool #20, *The 70% Rule, or Why 7 Is the New 10.*
- Clients who find *Sharing Gratitude* useful may also connect with the following practices that center on different forms of appreciation and thankfulness:
  - Tool #22, *The G.L.A.D. Technique*
  - Tool #23, *Here and Now Pleasantness*
  - Tool #26, *Savoring Success—Past, Present, and Future*

HANDOUT: SHARING GRATITUDE

Instructions:

Have you experienced gratitude today? Gratitude comes from the ancient word *gratitudo*, which means to find what is pleasing or to give thanks, as well as being related to the blessing at mealtime. The benefit of gratitude is that it cultivates a sense of openness, appreciation, altruism, and kindness. In a very real sense, gratitude is the tow truck big enough to pull you out of those deep life ruts.

Gratitude is surprisingly easy to do. It depends on where you place your attention. This is your choice: You can focus on what is missing in your life, or you can focus on what is present. As a wise sage once said, "Pray for what you already have in your life and you'll never be disappointed."

Follow along with the *Sharing Gratitude* worksheet and you can track how well this practice works for you.

Step 1. Familiarize Yourself with Gratitude

To help you get started, look over the two categories of gratitude that you can reflect upon. As you look over this list, you might imagine what life would be like without tapping into gratitude.

BASIC DAILY GRATITUDE

Roof over your head	Transportation for getting around	Bed to sleep in
Sunlight	Health	Ability to smile
Running water	Furniture where you live	Chairs to sit in
Food to eat	Coffee/Tea to drink	Trees
Smiling	The five senses	Electricity
Light bulbs	Supportive people in your life	Clothing

PARADOXICAL GRATITUDE

Paradoxical gratitude consists of finding gratitude for the circumstance you prefer *not* to have in your life. Think of whatever you are not happy with. For example, one could be dissatisfied or unhappy with any of the following: One's car, relationship, living conditions, job, career choice, family, friends, earnings, retirement, vacation plans, a recent loss, etc.

Whichever of these you may be unhappy about, consider why there is still something for which to be grateful. Suppose that your car broke down, but you can still afford to pay for a mechanic to fix it. Perhaps you lost a friendship or other important relationship, but you still could be grateful for others who support you during the loss. Or, you might be grateful for new doors that may open after a loss—those silver linings that none of us are ever prescient enough to predict!

By doing this you have discovered the secret of paradoxical gratitude!

Step 2. Journal Your Gratitude

Use a journal, your mobile device, or an index card to keep track of your gratitude. Each day for the next week, write down from 1-3 things you are grateful for that day. This can be a basic gratitude or a paradoxical gratitude, or both. By the way, having gratitude for just one thing is good enough—even if it turns out to be one item you are grateful for during the entire week.

Step 3. Share Your Gratitude

Keeping a gratitude journal is nice because it builds up the storehouse of memories about gratitude. But why not take gratitude a step further by sharing it with others. Sharing gratitude helps you connect with others around something that is positive and life-affirming.

Sharing your gratitude with others can be done in a number of ways. Here are a few suggestions:

- Begin by sharing your gratitude, then ask others (at the office, at home, at school, etc) what *they* have gratitude for. Let yourself open to the deeper ideas that grow out of this mutual discussion for finding meaning in life.
- Write a gratitude letter to someone who has done something helpful, kind, caring, impactful, or compassionate for you. Then, after writing your letter of thanks, share this letter with that individual. You can either present the letter to them, or you can share your gratitude in person.
- Share the story behind one of the things you are grateful for with another person.

Reflections: At the end of the week, look back over your gratitude journal or list. Do you notice a common theme? How does it feel to look this over? Does anything you wrote down surprise you? Finally, write down how you can continue to use gratitude and what your commitment is to this practice.

_____

_____

_____

_____

_____

_____

_____

Tool #22
The G.L.A.D. Technique

LEARNING STYLES

All learning styles are compatible with this gratitude-related practice:

Verbal-Linguistic

Visual-Spatial

Musical-Sound

Bodily-Kinesthetic-Tactile

Mathematical-Science-Logical

Social-Interpersonal

Reflective-Intrapersonal

Natural World

Existential-Meaning

THOUGHTS FOR THERAPISTS

When thinking of gratitude, I often recall the sentiments that Robert Louis Stevenson shared in a letter to a friend. He wrote: "It is the history of our kindnesses that alone makes this world tolerable. If it were not for that, for the effect of kind words, kind looks, kind letters . . . I should be inclined to think our life a practical jest in the worst possible spirit."

It's all too easy to minimize the importance of kindness; yet it is invaluable to notice. During a workshop, a mental health professional shared with the group the story of how she lost her wallet while attending a psychology conference in New York. She returned to the hotel very upset, and when a colleague suggested that she try gratitude, she said that she felt like bopping this person on the head! From her room, she started the long process of tracking down and calling the credit card companies to cancel her lost cards. At some point during that process, she realized how all those persons helping her were exceedingly kind, supportive, and understanding. Touched by the kindness of others, there came the realization that she could have gratitude for that. This quickly shifted her mood from being stuck in negativity and into a place of thankfulness and acceptance. About 10 minutes after completing the calls to cancel her cards, the phone rang. The front desk said she had a visitor. Being from out of town she didn't recognize the name, but she went down to the lobby anyway. Standing there was the man whose cab she had been in earlier that evening. The cabbie was holding her wallet, which she had left in the back seat. This is not to say that embracing gratitude will make things turn out as well as this—but it can shift one's mood dramatically.

The *G.L.A.D Technique* is a tool that I developed for clients or others stuck in rumination or facing depressive symptoms. It is designed as a means to expand upon the strengths of kindness and gratitude by noticing a myriad of other things in life that can provide a sense of worth, meaning, and appreciation. Each of the items in the *G.L.A.D. Technique* turns attention away from depressive, negative thoughts and toward something positive. Doing this practice over and over actually rewires the brain to look outward and locate what is pleasant in life.

TIPS FOR WORKING WITH CLIENTS

- *The G.L.A.D. Technique* can be applied in tandem with Tool #21, *Sharing Gratitude*. These two practices fit together very well.
- The G.L.A.D. practice is portable. Make a point of problem-solving with clients how they can use this practice on a daily or weekly basis.
- Have clients bring in their G.L.A.D. journal to share the stories of what they noticed and how it affected their mood.

HANDOUT: THE G.L.A.D. TECHNIQUE

Instructions:

G.L.A.D. is an acronym for ways of finding joy and balance. It works by paying attention to certain positive aspects of life that are around you all the time, but which frequently go unnoticed. Sound easy? It is!

To begin, look over each of the letters to get familiar with what each stands for. Then, use the guidelines below for starting your own G.L.A.D. practice.

G–One **Gratitude** that you're thankful for today
- This can represent the most *basic gratitude*, such as having food and water, sunlight, a body that works well enough, a roof over your head, etc.
- Your gratitude might also be about appreciating those truly significant things in your life—such as a devoted relationship, meaningful work, a caring community of friends, and robust health that allows you to experience life to the fullest, etc.

L–One new thing you **Learned** today
- This can be something you learned about yourself today, such as noticing an insight or wisdom that you possess.
- It could mean having an open attitude so that you can discover something new and interesting about another person (even someone you have known for a long, long time).
- This might just have to do with learning a new fact or gaining a new perspective on something—and that might make you happy because it is fun to be curious and to learn.

A–One small **Accomplishment** you did today
- Often, we mistakenly believe that an accomplishment has to be something super-sized. In truth, an accomplishment can be that ordinary act of self-care that you did for yourself or another. Examples might be:
  - Getting enough sleep.
  - Not skipping meals and getting enough nourishment.
  - Getting dressed in the morning (highly underrated!).
  - Doing anything that moves you (even slightly) toward reaching a long-term goal.

D–One thing of **Delight** that touched you today
- Consider anything that makes you laugh, smile, or brings you joy.
- This can be a thing of beauty that you notice during the day.
  - Examples could be hearing a bird chirp, seeing a colorful flower, laughing at a funny joke, tasting food, returning a smile, noticing the pleasant sensation of water on your hands while washing the dishes, etc.

G.L.A.D. Practice Guidelines:

Use a journal, mobile device, or an index card to keep track of those G.L.A.D. items that you notice. To really get in the practice, try to do this each day for the next week. If possible, try to notice an entirely new and unique gratitude, learning, accomplishment, and delight for each day.

While you can do this daily, you can also do a G.L.A.D. practice on a weekly basis. The important thing is that you write these down and keep them to look at in the future. One idea is to keep your G.L.A.D. items on an index card or some other portable device so that you can write these down the moment you notice them.

At the end of the week, look over your G.L.A.D. writings and answer the following questions:

Reflections: Congratulations on following through on your G.L.A.D. practice! What was it like to focus your attention in this way? How did it make you feel to start noticing these aspects of daily life?

_____

_____

_____

_____

Name one small way in which this practice benefitted you or someone in your life?

_____

_____

_____

_____

How could you share your G.L.A.D. ideas with others? What is the most effective method (daily, weekly) for you to continue using the G.L.A.D. Technique?

_____

_____

_____

_____

Tool #23
Here and Now Pleasantness

LEARNING STYLES

This practice encourages individuals to find pleasantness that is around them by using the entire palette of learning styles:

Verbal-Linguistic

Visual-Spatial

Musical-Sound

Bodily-Kinesthetic-Tactile

Mathematical-Science-Logical

Social-Interpersonal

Reflective-Intrapersonal

Natural World

Existential-Meaning

THOUGHTS FOR THERAPISTS

Here and Now Pleasantness is a simple practice that engages focused attention in a way that turns one's focus away from negative thoughts while placing it squarely on whatever happens to be comforting and soothing. The fact that this awareness practice is deceptively easy to use is one of its greatest advantages. There's very little one needs to do except put on the filter of pleasantness. Through this filter, a different experience appears and, in some cases, this can be very profound.

Consider, for example, the true story of individual with severe depression who learned this practice in a therapy session. Upon returning the next week, he was asked to recount his experience of here and now pleasantness. He responded that he heard a bird chirping, which reminded him of springtime, and then said, "And that gave me hope." Most likely, the chirping bird was there all along. All that was needed was to put on the filter of pleasantness to give this patient an entirely new perspective.

TIPS FOR WORKING WITH CLIENTS

- Use the *Here and Now Pleasantness* handout as a readable script from which you can guide clients through the process, as well as giving them the handout.

- A practice that matches well with *Here and Now Pleasantness* is Tool #25, *My Favorite Things*. When used together, these will present many opportunities for rewiring attention in a positive way.

- *Here and Now Pleasantness* helps someone tap into existing learning styles. If someone is visual, for example, that person is more likely to notice colors or objects. By noticing what a client chooses, you will get a clearer picture of their learning style.

- Pleasantness is portable. The key for clients is helping them to remember to use this throughout the day.

- Suggest clients tap into pleasantness each time they change locations or environments. This way, they are repeatedly focusing on pleasantness time and time again, which is an effective means for creating a new, healthy coping skill.

HANDOUT: HERE AND NOW PLEASANTNESS

Instructions:

This is an easy to use practice that can help you go off auto-pilot and really notice your environment in greater detail. In particular, you are going to use it to notice positive and pleasant things that are all around you. To practice this, it is best to be seated in a place where you are not going to be distracted or interrupted.

When you're settled and ready, follow along with this short script:

Right now, look around the room or space that you are in. This could be the therapy room, a room where you live, or any location—even outside.

With a sense of childlike curiosity, look around and find one item that is pleasant, or pleasing, to you. It could be a color, a shape, an object, a sound, a smell, or a texture of something that you can touch. Be sure to examine the entire space around you. If you're in a room, tilt your head up to look at the ceiling, then down the walls, and all the way down to the floor. Don't let anything go unnoticed! Once you find something pleasant, spend some time thinking about what you like about it. By the way, if you happen to notice multiple pleasant items, that's okay too.

Looking at the object you find pleasant, ask yourself: What is it exactly that I like about it? Is it the shape, the size, or the color of it? Does it remind me of a pleasant or happy memory?

It is very common for the practice of Here and Now Pleasantness to elicit positive and enjoyable memories. For example, you might find a curved shape that reminds you of a wave of water curling in the ocean. Or, you may find that a color or object reminds you of a favorite season of the year or some other positive memory. Whatever your memory may be, allow yourself to savor it for as long as you want.

After you have experienced a pleasant object, sound, or sight, etc., go and find another in the room or space around you. Again, pay attention to why you like it. Sometimes, you may notice a favorite color or sound that just makes you feel good.

Good job on locating pleasantness right here, right now! Answer the reflections that follow to think about how you can use this on a daily basis.

Reflections: How did putting on the filter of "here-and-now pleasantness" make you feel? Did you notice that it helped to shift the mind away from busy or "unpleasant" thoughts?

_____

_____

_____

_____

The *Here and Now Pleasantness* practice doesn't take up any space in your purse or wallet, so you can use it anywhere you happen to be. How could this practice help you be more aware and present in your surroundings?

_____

_____

_____

_____

Guidelines for Using *Here and Now Pleasantness*:   Each time you move from one place to another, or each time you walk through a doorway and enter a new room or space, make it a point of activating *Here and Now Pleasantness* to find one new pleasant thing.

Now that you've successfully completed this practice, you can again look for pleasantness the moment you step outside. Look around and see if there's some kind of pleasantness that you missed earlier in the day. Even if you drive the same route to work each day, work in the same space day after day, or live in the same room, you can look for something new—as well as re-experience something as pleasant over and over again in this moment.

Do this often enough, and you will rewire your brain by repeatedly entering the *Here and Now Pleasantness* before you. Enjoy the view.

Tool #24
Change Your (History) Channel

THOUGHTS FOR THERAPISTS

Have you ever known someone who was stuck on the history channel? Who kept repeating the same story like a recording that was looped over and over? It happens, and it is especially understandable when trauma and abuse are involved. As therapists, this tells us a lot about how such an individual may be living out that old story each day. In his book *Healing the Mind Through the Power of Story*, narrative psychiatrist Lewis Mehl-Madrona writes, "We live by enacting the stories we believe to be true."

Mehl-Madrona and others have written about the benefit of widening out attention by broadening out the stories we tell. In particular, stories can serve to redefine our problems, organize us toward feeling states, and support a feeling of security and safety. This works because the brain is fundamentally symbolic and wired for finding meaning through storytelling.

TIPS FOR WORKING WITH CLIENTS

- Help clients think of the old history channel story in a new way by looking at the strengths that it displays. This strengths perspective can help clients to rewrite, or revise, the old story.

- Consider combining this exercise with Tool #27, *Strengths Journal*, as a way to redefine and broaden one's story by focusing on endearing (and enduring) personal qualities and abilities.

- Guide clients toward finding a story that supports a feeling of safety and calm.

- A good mindfulness exercise could be to have clients track, or count, the number of times in a day that they tell themselves the history channel story. At such times, they can redirect awareness or refer to the handout.

HANDOUT: CHANGE YOUR (HISTORY) CHANNEL

Instructions:

Our personal stories play a significant role in our lives, but if an old (and perhaps painful) story has been playing in your head for a long time, then it might be time to find a different story to focus on—or at the very least, take a break from the old story so you can get a breather! While the old story is there for a reason (and you can always choose to return to it at anytime), it's essential to know that you also have the *choice* to revise the old story, or find other valid stories that help you recognize your strengths and feel more in charge of your life.

The purpose of this handout is to help you become aware of your stories and think about using them in a new way. The following questions will guide you through the process of exploring and considering new ways of dealing with an old, repeating story. Remember, too, that this is just one approach for dealing with the old story. There are many methods for reappraising and releasing the pain of trauma or abuse.

What follows are six different practices for investigating your stories in new ways. As you use each practice, think of it as putting the TV remote in your hand. Each method gives you a way to click the remote and switch from the old story (or history channel) to a new one whenever you want to. Happy story-creating and story-telling!

Practice 1: Count the Old Story and Refocus Away from It

Have you ever thought of counting the number of times that the old, unhappy story comes up during the course of a day?

a) **For the next seven days, keep track of your old stories (on a sheet of paper, mobile device, etc). Each time the story appears to you, mark this down.**

Also, just because a thought or story pops up in your head doesn't mean that you need to respond to it. Like a broken record, you can lift the needle off the record player and put on a new tune!

b) **After you count the story, change the channel to a different, more supportive story by using one or more of the following practices.**

Don't worry how many times the old story comes up. Just work on changing the channel when it does.

Practice 2: Find Supportive Stories of Safety and Calm

Spend some time to think about a story from your past where you felt safe, secure, and calm. Maybe you were with someone who made you feel safe—even if it was a grade school teacher, grandparent, or friend. Write the story down below. Remember it in as much detail as possible. Even if it represents a small event, allow yourself to savor, enjoy, and re-experience it. Be sure to include the sights, sounds, smells, and sensations of that safe and calm memory.

_____

_____

_____

_____

_____

_____

Practice 3: Recall Stories of Strength, Resilience, and Hope

For this practice, you are going to think back on those times where you experienced or displayed strength, resilience, and hope. Remember, too, that even a difficult story can display your strengths. Strengths can take many forms, and do not need to follow along with a traditional idea of strength. Patience, quiet, hospitality, compassion, caring, listening, sharing, and acceptance are all examples of personal strengths.

For a resilience story, think of a time that you bounced back from a difficult life situation. The fact that you are working this exercise is itself a sign of resilience!

A hope story can be anytime that you move toward a goal, sought out resources and advice from others, or shared hope with others who needed it.

Write down ideas relating to these stories in the space below. If you need more space, complete this practice on a separate sheet of paper.

_____

_____

_____

_____

_____

_____

_____

_____

Practice 4: Find Books, Films, and Stories that You Love

Do you have a favorite story that you have read over and over? Is there a movie that makes you feel hopeful or connects with you in some deep way? Is there a children's story that makes you brighten and smile? Write down your favorites below.

In addition, include the strengths of the characters in those stories. Many children's books, for example, are about strengths that a character in the story is trying to find. What draws you to these characters? What do you admire most about them? How do you reflect those very strengths in your own life story?

_____

_____

_____

_____

_____

_____

_____

Practice 5: Find a Neutral Story

Sometimes we can broaden our attention, or turn away from the old history channel story simply by finding a nice, old-fashioned boring story! This like the story where you go to the store to pick up groceries and nothing very exciting happens. But nothing bad or dramatic happens either—which is a good thing.

This is another strategy for using your remote to change the channel. Simply click and go to a story where you felt no strong emotion, one way or the other. See what it's like to change to this channel. Write down one or more of those boring stories below.

_____

_____

_____

_____

_____

_____

_____

Practice 6: Journal What It Was Like to Change Your History Channel

At the end of the week, reflect back on your experiences with changing the history channel. Over the period of a week, did it become easier to change the channel? Was there a change in the frequency of the old story as the days went by? Which practice(s) for changing the channel worked best for you? How could you continue to use these?

_____

_____

_____

_____

_____

_____

Which of the six practices for changing the channel worked best for you? How could you continue to use these?

_____

_____

_____

_____

_____

_____

_____

Tool #25
My Favorite Things

THOUGHTS FOR THERAPISTS

Everyone, it seems, has favorite things that can shift their awareness and improve their mood. In conducting workshops around the country, I have found that one of the more popular exercises is the practice of *My Favorite Things*. This practice borrows its name from the timeless Rodgers and Hammerstein song whose lyrics tell the story of remembering favorite things in order to avoid feeling bad.

My Favorite Things is a grounding activity for which there's no need to reinvent the wheel. This practice could just as easily be called *Finding Comfort with the Familiar*, because clients tailor this practice to whatever is comforting for them.

TIPS FOR WORKING WITH CLIENTS

- Exploring a client's past history regarding favorite hobbies and activities can provide insight into someone's list of favorites.
- One advantage of using *My Favorite Things* is that it doesn't require someone to actually perform an activity. Rather, it focuses on mental rehearsal, or visualization.
  - Consider bundling this practice with the following:
    - Tool #18, *Visualizing the Calm*
    - Tool#22, *The G.L.A.D. Technique*
- If you are working with substance abuse and PTSD, consider the book *Seeking Safety* by Lisa Najavits, which offers an integrated treatment approach that incorporates grounding methods.

HANDOUT: MY FAVORITE THINGS

Instructions:

Let's try an experiment. Right now, think of a favorite color. Focus on that favorite color for a few moments longer. Perhaps you are even wearing a blouse, shirt or other piece of clothing that contains that color. Close your eyes and picture this color in your mind's eye for a few more seconds before continuing on.

How did this favorite color focus your attention? How did you feel when paying attention to your favorite color?

The practice of *My Favorite Things* is like a giant magnet that attracts your attention by focusing you on things that you enjoy, that bring you a sense of comfort, and that help you feel secure. Best of all, you can tailor your favorites to match what you already enjoy.

PART 1: Create a *Favorite Things* List

Look at the list of words below. *You will use these to put together a list of categories to focus on.* Note that there are two categories: 1) a category for your single most favorite thing, and 2) a category for multiple items—so you can think about more than one favorite color, person, or place, etc. Circle the ones that instantly appeal to you. Don't think too hard about these.

Use this when you are feeling down, scattered, or experiencing negative thoughts.

Category 1—**Circle the categories where you can think of a single most favorite thing that makes you feel good.**

Feel-good song	Person	Visual artist or art work
Season	Healthy food	Color
Meal	Time of day	Snack food
Mobile app	Morning activity	Feel-good book
Magazine	Teacher	Family member
School subject	Hobby	Extreme sport
Sport	Sports team	Safe, relaxing place
Vacation spot	Room where I live	Historical figure
Comfort food	Comedian/joke	Contemplative practice
Tree	Flower	Scenic place
Park	Car/transportation	Album
Accomplishment	Gratitude	Smell/scent
Article of clothing	Fashion designer	Purse/wallet
TV show	Radio show	Celebrity

If you have other favorite things that are not mentioned in the list above, add your others here:

_____

_____

Now, compile the items you circled by writing them down in one place. Use an index card, sheet of paper, or computer, or phone to-do list. At the top of the list write: ***My Single Most Favorite Things***.

Category 2—**Circle the words where you easily have at <u>least two or more favorite things</u> in that category that make you feel good.**

Feel-good songs	People	Musical artists
Seasons	Healthy foods	Colors
Meals	Times of day	Snack foods
Mobile apps	Morning activities	Feel-good books
Magazines	Teachers	Family members
School subjects	Hobbies	Extreme sports
Sports	Sports teams	Safe, relaxing places
Vacation spots	Rooms where I live	Historical figures
Comfort foods	Comedians/jokes	Contemplative practices
Trees	Flowers	Scenic places
Parks	Cars/transportation	Albums
Accomplishments	Gratitudes	Smells/scents
Articles of clothing	Fashion designers	Purses/wallets
TV shows	Radio shows	Celebrities

Now, compile this list of categories on an index card, sheet of paper, computer, or phone to-do list. At the top of this list write: ***My Many Favorite Things***.

PART 2: Access Your Favorite Things List

Use either or both of these favorite lists anytime you need to counterbalance rumination, or when you feel overwhelmed by chaos and stress. Use these guidelines to help you successfully use the *My Favorite Things* practice:

GUIDELINES:
- Practice going over your favorites list for 10 minutes or longer. Get familiar with how long it takes for you to feel calm or uplifted.
- You can use this practice anytime, but it may be most effective if you start focusing on your favorites before you reach a high level of negativity or feel extremely stressed or depressed.
- Consider using *My Favorite Things* as a preventive technique, such as prior to entering a situation or circumstance that has acted as an emotional trigger in the past.
- If possible, find a quiet place where you can go to focus on *My Favorite Things*. You may only need a few minutes to get centered.
- Go through your list, starting from the top. Focus on as many details of each favorite thing as you can. For example, if it's a song, sing the song in your head. If it's a favorite book, imagine your favorite characters and favorite parts of the book. If it's a favorite scenic place, try to recall everything you can about that place by using all of your senses.
- Continue going through one or both lists for as long as needed, or until you feel grounded, safe, and calm.

Tool #26
Savoring Success—Past, Present, and Future

THOUGHTS FOR THERAPISTS

In the book *Savoring: A New Model of Positive Experience*, authors Fred Bryant and Jean Veroff explore how one's mood can be shifted in a positive direction by intentionally basking in the warm memories and feelings associated with past successes. All that's needed is mental focus and re-experiencing what once gave us a feeling of pride or positive self- esteem.

What's more, the practice of savoring is flexible enough to spread joy and wonder across time, because it can be used to reflect upon the past, consider present-moment joy, and even anticipate future pleasurable experiences.

Savoring is more than a positive psychology concept. It is a mindful awareness practice that lets us choose where to direct our awareness. In this case, the choice is to turn the mind away from negativity and toward pleasantness and positivity. This is not to say, of course, that negative experiences are invalid or lack meaning or potential for growth, but that to dwell *only* on the negative is not a fair appraisal of our total life experience. To savor is to bring greater balance and wholeness into one's life.

TIPS FOR WORKING WITH CLIENTS

- Consider using the *Savoring Success—Past, Present, and Future* handout in conjunction with the following chapters:
  - Tool #16, *BE-THIS Sense-Grounding*, which also incorporates the idea of labeling thoughts and sensations.
  - Tool #24, *Change Your (History) Channel*, which reframes and broadens a negative narrative by finding a more positive one.
- Have clients practice *Savoring Success* in session when they first learn about it.

- The practice of savoring is very adaptable. Because older adults often associate tranquility and contentment with life satisfaction, try adapting the exercise as follows:
  - Use tranquility as the focus of a savoring practice.
  - Have the client assemble a list of those ways they feel content, in order to enhance the experience of a well lived life.

- A savored memory does not have to be of a major accomplishment, but even one small thing that someone is proud of, such as learning a skill or performing an action that required perseverance and tenacity.

- Focusing on a memory of being a benefactor and helping others has been shown to increase prosocial behavior and enhance positive affect.
  - Reflecting on the act of assisting others can establish one's identity as someone who is caring and capable.

- When anticipating a future event, it is important for the client not to over-exaggerate an upcoming experience, but to be realistic in their anticipation.
  - Clients can base anticipation of a future experience on an enjoyable past experience which is similar to the one they are planning.

HANDOUT: SAVORING SUCCESS—PAST, PRESENT, AND FUTURE

Savoring is a practice for really steeping yourself—for several minutes at a time—in a pleasurable or positive memory or experience. It can help you reminisce about a past success in your life, allow you to more deeply enjoy what is right around you this moment, and let you positively anticipate an upcoming event. In other words, savoring is a tool for getting you feeling better by recognizing the positives in your life—whether past, present, or future.

Ideally, you can blend all three types of savoring. And as you start your savoring practice you will gain more awareness and experience for fully enjoying all parts of your life. In this way you can honor your history, appreciate the now, and bring an attitude of eagerness for what is to come.

This exercise includes three different ways to savor. After you familiarize yourself with these, follow the instructions for each. Try all of these methods of shifting mental gears. Now, let's get ready to savor.

1. Savoring Past Successes

Reminiscing about one of your past successes can produce a feeling of well-being. For this kind of savoring you will reflect on the following kinds of past experiences:

- Any experience that made you feel proud, such as—
  - A past accomplishment (finishing a class, completing a project at home or work, cooking or preparing a new recipe, etc).
  - Any action of kindness, caring, or compassion that helped someone to feel grateful, or which benefitted another person. This can also include the action of volunteering for a beneficial cause.
  - Any action that moved you toward a long-term goal, no matter how small.

Instructions:

1) Think of a past memory that fits one of the categories above. The idea here is to savor your past experience for an extended period of time.

2) Find a quiet place where you can mentally savor all the details of your past success.

3) Spend at least 5 minutes mentally recalling a favorite memory of a success, how it made you feel proud, as well as how you felt joyful. If others shared in your joy and success, imagine them as well. Steep yourself in the experience, as if you are experiencing it for the very first time. Remember, you can savor the same experience over and over, or you can find other memories and categories and practice savoring them as well.

4) Optionally, you can journal your savoring experience for five minutes. Use the space below, or use a separate sheet.

_____

_____

_____

_____

_____

_____

_____

_____

_____

_____

_____

_____

_____

_____

_____

2. Savoring Present Experiences

Focusing on your present moment experience goes beyond simply trying to find pleasure. The practice of being engaged, focused, and present is in itself a steadying and soothing sensation. With this kind of awareness, you can practice being present during any of the following conditions:

• Any distraction that takes you away from the activity you are engaged in.

• Any external annoyance or irritation that captures your attention.

• Any internal negative or anxious thought that you are dwelling on.

• Any obsessive thought or craving sensation in the body.

Instructions:

1) Throughout the day, get in the habit of asking yourself this question: *Where is my mind right now?* Wherever your mind might be, you can simply notice where it has wandered.

2) When you find your mind has taken a little trip away from the activity you are engaged in, just label that as "mind-wandering," "thinking," or "mental sensation." If your mind has been drawn to a mental image, you can simply label that as "seeing." Likewise, if a sound has taken you out of this moment, you can label that as "hearing," then return to the present activity.

3) After labeling your mind's wandering, you can let go of the thought (visual image or other sensation that has grabbed you) and redirect your mind to pay attention to this present moment and to return to the body. You will also return to the activity you were engaged in during your moment of mind-wandering.

4) When you come back to the present, notice as much as you can about what you are doing. Spend up to five minutes being present in the following ways, allowing yourself to be focused and engaged with whatever you are doing. See how this present moment state of awareness brings a pleasant or centered feeling.

   - If you are moving your body, appreciate how the body follows your command. Marvel in the dexterity of your body, your hands, and other movement. Notice the colors and shapes around you, taking care to notice any favorite colors or objects. For example, if you are sitting at the computer, you can notice how your hands rest on the keyboard, the colors on the screen, and how your body feels in the chair.

   - Turn your attention toward something for which you can be grateful which is in your environment or the activity in which you are engaged. That could be anything from having a roof over your head to the warm cup of coffee or tea on your desk, to appreciating the clothes that you wear or the comfortable chair that you sit in.

5) Optionally, after getting into the "pleasant present," spend a little longer to journal your savoring the present experience. Use the space below to do this.

_____

_____

_____

_____

_____

_____

_____

_____

_____

_____

_____

_____

_____

_____

3. Savoring Future Experiences

Anticipating the future can stimulate a positive feeling. The idea is not to idealize the future, but to realistically savor those aspects of it that you can expect to find pleasant. The future is unlimited as far as the kinds of experiences you can eagerly anticipate. Here are just a few:

- Projects that you have planned for your home, work, family, friends, etc.
- Relationship-oriented activities, including everything from meeting a friend or family member for dinner and planning a party to thinking about a future vacation or trip.
- Personal experiences that are related to goal-setting, such as exercising and getting in shape, social engagements, and engaging in hobbies.

Instructions:

1) Think of a future event that fits one of the categories above. You can spend time anticipating the actual event, or even allow yourself to thoroughly enjoy the planning process. If you're planning an event, consider starting early so you will have more time to get excited about it and savor it.

2) Find a quiet place where you can mentally imagine the details of what you will find pleasurable about your upcoming event. Focus only on those aspects of it that you know you are likely to enjoy.

3) Spend at least five minutes visualizing the future event or experience. If it is a social situation, imagine those with whom you will be interacting in a fun and pleasurable way. Immerse yourself in this visualization, employing all your senses to see, hear, feel, and smell all that you can appreciate in the environment you will be encountering.

If this event is something you are in the process of planning, allow yourself to savor the planning process. Enjoy the preparation, making sure you visualize how your planning will produce the outcome you are hoping for.

Here's a tip: When anticipating a future event, try to be realistic about the pleasure and joy you will experience from it. You might draw upon a similar experience from your past to help you do this. A realistic approach will help to ensure that the future experience you're savoring will exceed your imagination, not be underwhelming or disappointing!

4) Optionally, you can journal your anticipation of a future experience. Use the space below to do this.

_____

_____

_____

_____

_____

_____

_____

_____

_____

_____

_____

Reflections: Which of the savoring methods—past, present, or future—worked best for you? What was it that you liked most about this practice?

_____

_____

_____

_____

There are other ways to adapt the practice of savoring. For example, you can savor the times in your life that you felt tranquil or content—recalling these in detail. You can also make a list of the ways in which you feel content in your life right now. How do you think that increasing your awareness of contentment or tranquility would enhance your sense of living a life well lived? If you feel this would be satisfying, focus on tranquility or contentment the next time you use savoring.

_____

_____

_____

_____

Tool #27
Identifying Strengths & Strengths Journal

THOUGHTS FOR THERAPISTS

Identifying strengths is like putting on a new pair of sunglasses. Looking through the lens of strengths can dramatically alter our view, color our experiences, and bring a new sense of confidence, well-being, and self-esteem.

In the article, "A dynamic approach to psychological strength development and intervention"—published in *The Journal of Positive Psychology*—authors Robert Biswas-Diener, Todd Kashdan, and Gurpal Minhas promote the concept of 'strengths development.' "Strengths," they write, "are not fixed traits across settings and time (the dominant, contemporary approach to personality). Instead, we adopt dynamic, within-person approaches . . . Strengths are potentials for excellence that can be cultivated through enhanced awareness, accessibility, and effort."

This approach is an exciting and empowering one, because it puts the client squarely in the driver's seat, improving his or her sense of efficacy and self-esteem. Strangely, it seems easier for many to focus on weaknesses and flaws than on strengths. Whether this is just old conditioning or the stress core of the brain always focusing on the negative, focusing on strengths seems to be a palliative, an antidote to critical self-talk. The *Identifying Strengths & Strengths Journal* handout that follows is ideal for using in therapy, and it's a starting point for a long-term practice of noticing and recognizing one's personal, and perhaps, long-ignored strengths.

TIPS FOR WORKING WITH CLIENTS

- Adapt the handout by having the client share her or his story of coming to the therapy session that day. Then, you can identify the strengths you hear in that story.
- The *Strengths Journal* practice can be augmented by combining it with these two complementary chapters:
  - Tool #24, *Change Your (History) Channel*
  - Tool # 26, *Savoring Success, Past, Present, and Future*

- Be aware of the client's tendency to ignore strengths as just being part of their "routine." You can normalize this behavior by noting how easy it is to take strengths for granted.

- A client's resistance to admitting strengths may be related to that individual's underlying schema about self worth and adequacy.

- If someone can't accept a compliment or rejects the idea of strengths as phony or inauthentic, consider exploring their family history around accepting strengths.

- The handout is designed to identify what can be thought of as *ordinary, everyday strengths.*

- Two valuable resource books include my own book, *The Joy Compass*, which is filled with many strength-oriented exercises and concepts. Also consider *The Strengths Book* by Janet Willars, Robert Biswas-Diener, and Alex Linley, a book which explores 60 different strengths.

HANDOUT: IDENTIFYING STRENGTHS & STRENGTHS JOURNAL

Have you ever thought about the variety of personal strengths each of us possesses? Sure, it's easy to ignore our strengths when feeling down or just trying to put one foot in front of the other. Fortunately, the everyday, ordinary strengths we have been using can help us to feel stronger—once we start to notice them! Consider that without using daily, ordinary, everyday strengths, we probably would not get through the day!

If you had to name three of your top strengths, what comes to mind? Would you be surprised to learn that you have numerous strengths, maybe dozens?

Finding strengths is an ongoing practice. It's a very satisfying and realistic way of acknowledging our true selves—and viewing our experiences through a new set of lenses. Follow along with the instructions below to try on this unique pair of glasses.

Instructions:

Share your story of going to any recent appointment with another person (optionally, you can write the story down). Keep in mind that this can also be the story of going to work in the morning—even if you work out of the home.

For this story, you are going to go into detail regarding the following information:

<u>Your Personal History</u>—what history do you have about this particular appointment? If the appointment is early in the morning, do you have a history around getting up early, getting on the freeway, and dealing with traffic? Your history is anything from your past that is relevant to this appointment.

<u>Stressors</u>—what stressors had an impact on going to your appointment? Stressors relate to such things as your 1) **sleep** (did you get an adequate amount of sleep the night before), 2) **nutrition** (did you eat or skip breakfast, lunch, etc), 3) **body** (tiredness, hunger, illness, pain), 4) **mood** (mood and/or thoughts that affected your ability to get to your appointment), 5) **habits** (behaviors that either supported or made getting to your appointment more difficult), and 6) **responsibilities** (obligations related to others or yourself that you needed to attend to).

<u>PART 1:</u>   Now, share this story with another, or write it in the space below.

_____

_____

_____

_____

_____

_____

_____

_____

_____

_____

_____

PART 2: *Identify and circle your strengths* using the list below. Remember that recognizing your strengths is not a form of bragging, but a way of realistically noticing where you are skillful and effective. This is not a time for humility, so don't be shy about circling the strengths that are part of your story!

NOTE: If you are telling this story to another person, the listener does not interrupt, but listens with openness and empathy. After the story is completed, the listener's job is as follows: *To identify the strengths that are revealed in the story that is being told.* If it is helpful, the listener can also draw upon the list of 50 strengths noted below.

adventurous	authentic	concentration
eagerness	self-knowing insight	courageous
humility	charisma	collaborative
responsible	encouraging	persistent
service-oriented	compassionate	kind
caring	accessible	accepting
understanding	empathetic	loyal
hospitable to others	faithful	spontaneous
passionate	listening	contemplative
questioning	spiritual	religious
wise	playful	practical
curious	open	thoughtful
sensitive	dignified	dedicated
flexible	adaptive	balanced
perspective	prepared	purposeful
detailed	honest	trustworthy
patient	generous (with materials, time, & emotions)	

Reflections: How did it feel to identify—or have someone else identify—your strengths? Was it affirming, validating, or even empowering?

_____

_____

How could you start to identify strengths as you go through the day?

_____

_____

Consider starting a strengths journal as a way to acknowledge and honor your strengths on a daily basis. How would you go about undertaking this process? What strengths could you use to help you achieve this goal?

_____

_____

_____

Tool #28
Putting on Weather Gear

THOUGHTS FOR THERAPISTS

A sage once said, "It may be raining outside, but if you can get above the clouds it's always sunny." While we can't always get above the clouds, we can learn how to deal with the weather however messy it might be. This is an approach that requires awareness of the weather, as well as skills in choosing the right gear to help you get through until the bad weather passes.

Meditation teacher and author Eknath Easwaran once wrote, "The wind is always blowing, but we have to do the work of making our boat seaworthy." The weather as something that we can't always control is the metaphor, and the subject, of this handout.

TIPS FOR WORKING WITH CLIENTS

- Weather is an easy to use metaphor that depicts the conditions of someone's personal situation.
- Have clients rate their weather on a scale, such as 1-10 (10 the worst), as well as with words.
- Discuss in detail what kind of weather gear has worked for the client in the past.
- As alternate ways to deal with 'bad weather,' consider the following two approaches:
  - Tool #30, *Activating with Mental Rehearsal*
  - Tool #31, *The Lightness of Laughter*

HANDOUT: PUTTING ON WEATHER GEAR

Everyone has to deal with the weather. As we know, there are all kinds of bad weather to contend with, and the same is true in life. Fortunately, like the weather, the challenging life conditions we face are often temporary. Eventually, the sun shines again.

In this handout you will think about the kind of weather gear you can put on that will help you to deal with those unpredictable, stormy conditions you may face—regardless of how severe. There are two parts to this practice. Follow along with the instructions below.

PART 1: Give your detailed 'Weather Report.'

Instructions:

In the space below, write a few sentences to describe the weather in your life right now. Like your favorite seasoned weather forecaster, describe a weather system that is happening right now, or predict a future weather pattern that is headed your way.

As you do this, you can answer the following questions:

• What is the severity of the weather? What kind of storm is this? (thunderstorm, snow, ice, drizzling rain, tornado, hurricane, heat wave, drought, freezing temperatures, blizzard, sandstorm, etc).

• You can also rate this on a 1-10 scale, with 1 the most mild and 10 the most severe.

• Is this weather system slow moving or fast?

• For how long a period of time do you expect this weather will last?

• Is the weather a prediction of what is to come? What kind of weather do you forecast and why?

_____

_____

_____

_____

_____

_____

_____

_____

PART 2: Describe the 'Weather Gear' necessary to protect you from the weather.

Instructions:

In the space below, explore the weather gear that can help you successfully get through either a mild weather system or avoid the damaging consequences of a severe storm.

Gear can be anything from an umbrella and raincoat to a down jacket and the refuge of a storm shelter. After choosing your weather gear, describe how this weather gear translates into real life skills or resources. For example, an umbrella to keep you dry from a dreary or persistent drizzle might be listening to uplifting music or having a meal with a good friend. Likewise, the refuge of a storm shelter might be finding those people or resources that can help you deal with your severe storm.

In as much detail you can, describe the weather gear you will need, what this will look like, and how effective you think it will be.

_____

_____

_____

_____

_____

_____

_____

_____

_____

Reflections: How does giving a weather report help clarify what you need to do to deal with this particular weather pattern or system?

_____

_____

_____

_____

_____

_____

How helpful is it to know that the weather is temporary? How accurate are you at predicting future weather? How can you use your time to better prepare for upcoming storms?

_____

_____

_____

_____

_____

_____

Tool #29
Tune Up with Music

THOUGHTS FOR THERAPISTS

Music is ingrained in humans, and it has been highly valued throughout our history. Music possesses the enviable ability to rapidly shift moods and feelings. Daniel Levitin, who is a professor of both psychology and music, as well as author of *The World in Six Songs*, makes the point that music bolsters the immune system and modulates important neurotransmitters. In this way, music can uplift us, while at the same time creating a more flexible and positive mindset.

Music attunes us to the world and culture around us. Of course, different kinds of music can affect us in dramatically different ways. Music can calm and soothe, and there is even research showing that people who listen to soothing music after a surgical operation heal more quickly. The good news is that a heightened awareness of the role music plays in our lives can be tapped as a valuable therapeutic tool.

TIPS FOR WORKING WITH CLIENTS

- Invite a dialogue with clients about the importance of music in their lives. Other chapters that bring music into focus include the following:
  - Tool #25, *Finding Favorites*, which can feature a musical component.
  - Tool #49, *Healing with Music*
- Note the kind of music clients listen to when depressed—such as listening to sad love songs after a relationship break-up.
- Have clients make an inventory of what music makes them happy.
  - Explore what music helps tune out depression and tunes in feelings of happiness.

HANDOUT: TUNE UP WITH MUSIC

Music is like a powerful drug. Did you know, for example, that the right musician actually boost your immune system, raise your mood, and even promote healing after a surgery?

Sounds amazing, but the music that plays through your headset, computer, or other device can counteract feelings of depression and tune you into a happier state of mind. This handout will let you discover how music plays *you* as much as you play *it*.

Instructions:

You are going to create a *Music-Mood Inventory* in the space below. This is an opportunity for you to find out how music alters how you feel. To do this, you will rate your mood as you listen to different kinds of music. Experiment with different kinds of music and see how each shifts your mood.

MOOD BEFORE	TYPE OF SONG/MUSIC	MOOD AFTER
In this column, describe the activity you are engaged in **before** music. Rate mood on a 1-10 scale: 1=low mood; 10=high mood	Name of song and type of music	Rate your mood again **after** listening to music using the 1-10 scale.

Reflections: What did you discover about music as a way to manage moods? What type of music or songs were most effective in changing your moods?

_____

_____

_____

_____

Optional: Make a playlist for various kinds of activities, such as 1) Chore Playlist, 2) Confidence and Feel Good Playlist, 3) Getting-Out-of-the-House Playlist, and 4) Starting (or Finishing) a Project Playlist. What other playlists of songs could motivate you? Write those in the space below:

_____

_____

_____

_____

Tool #30
Activating with Mental Rehearsal

THOUGHTS FOR THERAPISTS

Mental rehearsal is a well-researched method for improving and practicing most any skill. Mental rehearsal, or visualization, is so effective that The Navy Seals use it as an essential part of their mind-training program—helping the recruits master difficult fitness drills. Sports professionals and others use it, too, as a means for gaining mastery over a wide variety of skills.

The good news is that mental rehearsal is easily adapted for negative moods. For those dealing with symptoms of depression, mental rehearsal can be used to get them out of the house, feeling more energetic, and actively engaged with others. Visualization only takes a few minutes to learn, and it's a good way to enhance motivation. From exercising to calling up a friend on the phone, this handout will readily provide a tool that is practical, portable, and potent.

TIPS FOR WORKING WITH CLIENTS

- When having clients try *Activating with a Mental Rehearsal* in session, make sure that they are not triggered in any way by having their eyes closed. If so, they can always picture the visualization with eyes wide open.

- To optimize visualization, it is best practiced for a minimum of at least two minutes at a time. Time this during the practice session.

- Make sure that clients see themselves *successfully completing* whatever visual activity they are undertaking.

- Ask clients to notice if there is any change in heart rate or respiration while they are doing their visualization. They may even notice muscle twitches or sense the body moving.
  - Experiencing physical changes is normal and happens frequently.
  - Physical sensations can serve as evidence that the body doesn't know the difference between actual practice or mental practice.

- Two additional, related tools that can assist in getting people to overcome procrastination, move forward, or initiate action are the following:
  - Tool #24, *Change Your (History) Channel*
  - Tool # 27, *Identifying Strengths & Strengths Journal*

HANDOUT: ACTIVATING WITH MENTAL REHEARSAL

Did you ever watch a basketball player at the free throw line? Before shooting the ball, they are visualizing and mentally picturing the movement of the body and the ball as it swishes through the hoop. Even the Navy Seals practice mental rehearsal, or visualization, as a tool to help them succeed at the highly challenging "pool competency" part of their training—when they must untangle their scuba breathing tubes underwater before surfacing! This is not an easy task, but mental rehearsal actually improves the pass rate because it prepares the Seal recruits in advance for what they need to do.

In the same way, you can use mental rehearsal to help you accomplish even the smallest but important goals that you may find difficult at this time. The mental rehearsal here is designed to give you energy. Later, you can start adapting this technique in ways described below.

Right now, let's start with a very simple visualization for feeling more energetic.

Instructions:

1) Find a quiet place where you can close your eyes for up to two minutes. (If you don't like closing your eyes for any reason, you can keep your eyes open).

2) To begin, think of an activity that has energized you in the past. This could be taking a brisk walk, hiking, swimming, jumping on a trampoline, riding a horse, jogging along the beach, or doing a familiar workout routine. You can also think of a non-physical activity that energizes you, such as writing a poem, sketching, or playing chess. Picture yourself in great detail performing this activity. Notice the surroundings, including all the sights, sounds, objects, and colors of your environment where you are engaging in this activity.

If you haven't done this activity for a long time, that doesn't matter. You can still picture yourself doing something that you enjoyed and which gave you energy in the past. When you visualize the activity, make sure to *picture yourself as successfully completing it*. Don't see yourself as stopping or feeling exhausted . . . after all it's only for two minutes!

3) As you visualize the activity, notice if you feel any physical sensations, such as your breath deepening, your heart rate increasing, sensations in your muscles, and your body moving slightly. This often happens, and it shows you why mental rehearsal is effective.

4) Use a timer to keep track of time. Set it for two minutes, close your eyes and begin.

Reflections: How did it feel to do this mental rehearsal? Do you feel energized? What did you notice in your breathing, heart rate or body?

_____

_____

_____

_____

_____

_____

If you have thought about exercising, how could you use this visualization practice as a two minute warm-up to get you motivated for the real thing?

_____

_____

_____

_____

_____

_____

Other possible applications for this practice include visualizations for leaving the house, meeting friends, or starting a project. Use the space below to write down how you could use visualization to move you toward a goal—in even one small, simple and realistic way.

_____

_____

_____

_____

_____

_____

_____

Section 4

MINDFULNESS TOOLS FOR STRESS

Tool #31
The Lightness of Laughter

THOUGHTS FOR THERAPISTS

Did you ever have the occasion to work with someone who had a case of 'terminal seriousness'—and maybe deep frown lines etched into his or her face? In many cases, humor is an antidote for overcoming negativity while invoking a more pliable and playful state of mind. Don't underestimate the power of humor as a therapeutic tool and a way of building a relationship with the client. What is more, there is a bountiful trove of research extolling laughter's benefits—for everything from depression and insomnia to scrubbing out the body's toxic stress hormones and boosting the immune system.

Many anthropologists believe that laughter serves as a way to reduce conflicts and increase social bonding in groups. Human babies, for example, have a laughter response that occurs as early as four months of age. One of the pioneers who applied humor to medicine was Norman Cousins, who experienced the benefits of laughing while fighting a debilitating illness for which he was given only six months to live. As documented in his path-breaking book *Anatomy of an Illness*, Cousins had a friend bring a film projector into his room (this was long before portable, mobile devices) and proceeded to watch Marx Brothers' films, because that's what tickled his funny bone. To his amazement, he found that 30 minutes of belly laughter gave him up to two hours of anesthetic pain-free relief during which he could sleep. Today, The Norman Cousins Center for Psychoneuroimmunology at UCLA continues his work in using proven behavioral methods for promoting healing and well-being.

To counselors and mental health professionals the idea of introducing laughter into the therapy office might raise some red flags. Using some of the tips below, as well as trusting in your own sense of humor can help you to tread cautiously, but confidently, onto this path. There is a reason, for example, why native traditions like the Navajo initiate their newborns with a laughter ritual and use laughter throughout the lifespan: Life can be difficult and laughter helps us (en)lighten up. The *Lightness of Laughter* handout demonstrates that laughter is both a valuable coping skill and a potent buffer against stress.

TIPS FOR WORKING WITH CLIENTS

- It's important for clients to understand that humor neither trivializes nor minimizes the reasons they came to therapy.
  - Laughter provides another perspective; it does not erase or negate emotions like sadness, grief, or loss, etc., but lets us experience the fullness of all sides of life.
- The following chapters could be used as follow-up practices for exploring humor more deeply:
  - Tool #25, *My Favorite Things* could be used to find humorous things.
  - Tool #38, *Share an Uplifting and Hopeful Story* could be adapted as *Share an Uplifting and Funny Story.*
- It may be helpful to ask a client the question: *I'm curious—when was the last time you had a good belly laugh?*
  - This can lead to learning about the client's history around laughter, and how motivated they are to engage in laughter or humor. It may also provide insight into why they may have *stopped* laughing.
- Introduce clients to the extensive research on the benefits of laughter (see bibliography/resources for the LaughterYoga.org website and research findings.)
  - Humor has been shown to have therapeutic benefits.
- If you are naturally humorous, then your ability to connect through laughter is a way of being authentic with your client.

HANDOUT: THE LIGHTNESS OF LAUGHTER

Use this handout to examine and explore how you can bring the healing salve of laughter into your life. Laughter might not make your problem disappear, but it can help you to think differently about your problem by helping you think more clearly. Who knows?—it may even help you find a totally different perspective.

Studies on laughter show that having a more cheerful disposition can help us live longer, too, as well as helping improve sleep and lessen depression. Follow along with the four-part practice below for lightening your load.

Instructions:

PART 1:   In the space below, make a list of *Those Things that I Spend Too Much Time Worrying About.*

Examples of these include: things that push your buttons, critical comments (from yourself or others), what others think, bad drivers, personal demands, expectations from others, bad and insensitive bosses, and lack of control over certain situations or aspects of your life.

_____

_____

_____

_____

_____

_____

_____

_____

Reflections: What was it like to notice those buttons? How long have these been with you? How would it feel like to respond differently to these—and not let them get to you?

_____

_____

_____

_____

_____

_____

_____

_____

_____

PART 2: Make an executive decision to laugh it off! Let it go! Can you really decide to do that? Yes, of course you can! *Who* says you can't? *Why* can't you? Use the next minute to make that executive decision.

Reflections: How does it feel to make this kind of executive decision? What would it be like to continue to make this kind of executive decision the next time one of your buttons gets pushed? What would be the challenges you might face in doing this?

_____

_____

_____

_____

_____

_____

_____

PART 3: Write down the "lighter view" for each of the "buttons" or "serious thoughts" that confront you often. Be sure to include evidence that reacting and worrying about these is counterproductive for you.

_____

_____

_____

_____

_____

_____

_____

PART 4: Now it's time to explore just who and what makes you laugh. In the space below, write down all the persons or activities that make you feel "lighter." Who tickles that funny bone for you? This could be a family member or friend, comedian, neighbor, work associate, TV show, film, or book, etc. Make a point of spending time with these persons or activities. Use them as role models.

_____

_____

_____

_____

_____

_____

Reflections: How do you think inviting more humor into your life will change your experiences? How can you bring a little bit of laughter into your life each day?

_____

_____

_____

_____

_____

_____

Tool #32
The 'We' Cure

THOUGHTS FOR THERAPISTS

Without question, we very much live in a "me" culture. The Beatles even touched upon this focus long ago, in their song *I Me Mine*. Self-esteem, for example, can be considered the quest for a better and more likeable *me*. While self-esteem has its benefits, focusing *solely* within brings disadvantages. It can leave us with only half a life, disconnected from the vital life sustenance that comes from connecting deeply with others.

Psychological literature is replete with studies demonstrating the importance of supportive relationships. In a study titled "Social relationships and mortality risk: A meta-analytic review"—published in *PLOS Medicine*—researchers concluded that, "The influence of social relationships on risk for mortality is comparable with well-established risk factors for mortality." In fact, not having a positive social network was found to be as great a risk factor for early death as being alcoholic or smoking fifteen cigarettes a day; a poor social network was twice as risky as being obese.

Relating to others can benefit our health, but giving and volunteering on behalf of others goes a step further. It takes us out of ourselves and encourages a self-identity based on contributing to the world and others in a meaningful way. In fact, volunteering and giving to others has been shown to lift mood and influence prosocial behavior. This handout will help clients dissolve away their own stress by moving squarely from *me* to *we*.

TIPS FOR WORKING WITH CLIENTS

- *The 'We' Cure* handout can be done during a therapy session, and repeated as often as needed at home.
- There are two additional handouts that can be grouped with this one. Together, these combined approaches can help the client savor the deeper values of altruism, charity, and gratitude.

- #26, *Savoring Success—Past, Present, and Future*
- *Creating a Personal Intention Statement* (located in Tip #4, *Strengthening Intention and Attention*).

• It may be helpful to have the client notice any pleasant sensations in the body as they share a story about the time they may have helped another. It's useful for them to realize that helping 'feels good' at the body level.

• Some clients may feel that they can't measure up or do something that is truly beneficial or meaningful for another. In these cases, it can help to:
  - Normalize what it means to help others by depicting how even small, ordinary acts are good enough.
  - Share an example of someone whose *ordinary* acts of volunteerism added up over time, such as Mother Teresa.
  - Have the client reflect on one small action from another that was meaningful or beneficial to them.

HANDOUT: THE 'WE' CURE

This handout focuses on the power of being a *benefactor*. Benefactors are people who have the best interests of others in their hearts and minds.

You can probably recall a small act of kindness that affected you positively. Maybe it was that grade school teacher, a camp or school counselor, spiritual teacher, caring neighbor, loving grandparent, a friend, or other person who showed you that they cared. It could be the memory of an historical figure that performed kindly, enduring and endearing actions, like a Mother Teresa. (Believe it or not, the only thing that separates you from Mother Teresa is your next small, ordinary act of kindness—after all that's what she did, although she did it for years, which was truly *extraordinary*.)

In Part 1 of this two-part practice, you will first experience how good it feels to recall those times you have been a benefactor.

For Part 2, you will make a plan to be a benefactor. It's important to remember that you don't have to volunteer for a cause to do this.

Instructions:

PART 1:   For at least five minutes, use the space below to write about recent experiences in which you had a part in making others feel grateful. Choose any experience—at the workplace, at home, etc.—where your contribution or beneficial action causes others to feel gratitude and appreciation. Let go of any questioning about "whether my action measures up." *Any* action, no matter how small or insignificant it may seem to you, may be meaningful to others—especially if they have felt grateful for it! Write down the experience in great detail, remembering to write down how this experience made you feel.

_____

_____

_____

_____

_____

_____

_____

_____

_____

_____

_____

_____

_____

_____

_____

PART 2: In the space below, write down all the opportunities you may encounter during the upcoming week in which you could act as a benefactor. When you practice being a benefactor, you are expressing the simple wish for the well-being, happiness, safety, and health of others. How wonderful! You may also think about how being a benefactor connects to your deeper values, even your spiritual or religious path.

Leave no stone unturned as you explore and expand your benefactor capabilities—thinking about times and places where you could even act as a secret benefactor. Don't limit yourself as you do this exercise.

_____

_____

_____

_____

_____

_____

_____

_____

_____

_____

Reflections: How did it feel for you to consider expanding your benefactor experiences? What would it be like to create a *Benefactor Journal*? If you decide to do this, you can keep track of your benefactor activities, which will allow you to savor these experiences of contributing to others.

_____

_____

_____

_____

_____

_____

_____

_____

_____

_____

Tool #33
Squeeze Out Stress

THOUGHTS FOR THERAPISTS

Do we need to take stress seriously? We now know that stress does more than create havoc in the body and the immune system. The study, "Negative emotions in response to stress take a toll on long-term mental health"—published in *Psychological Science*—examined daily negative emotions caused by stress, as well as looked at mental health outcomes. Researchers found that not coping well with stress and holding onto negative emotions "predicted psychological stress (e.g., feeling worthless, hopeless, nervous, and/or restless) and diagnosis of an emotional disorder like anxiety or depression a full decade after the emotions were initially measured."

Since we can't eliminate sources of stress—neither could our ancestors for thousands of years—we need to find effective ways of coping with it. One method is progressive body relaxation, which has been used since the early 1920s as a way to manage external stressors that cause excessive tension in the body. In addition, there are many successful bio-feedback techniques and ways of measuring the reduction of stress. But the basic practice of relaxing the body is still one of the most effective and consistent ways of reducing stress. Plus, it is cost effective, portable, and doesn't require any fancy equipment.

Naturally, there are many variations on how to relax the body. Feel free to adapt this practice as needed to fit your client.

TIPS FOR WORKING WITH CLIENTS

- Use the handout instructions as a readable script to guide the client through this practice while in session. This is a good way to initially introduce the practice—rather than have the client read this while trying to follow along.
- One thing a client doesn't want to do is *try too hard* to relax!
  - Consider combining this practice with Tool #16, *B.E.-T.H.I.S. Sense Grounding*, which also teaches how to leave the busy mind behind and drop into the body.
  - Since this tool incorporates diaphragmatic breathing, you may want to also teach the client Tool #11, *The Power of Breath*.

- Tool #36, *"Breathing Into" Stress Detox* is another body-related practice that releases tension and tightness.

• It's important that the client practice this before the stress symptoms in the body get too intense, such as before the headache becomes a migraine or before the stomach pain becomes cramping or worse.

• As with any skill, the more one practices, the better this will work.
  - Consider having the client schedule practice periods—even when they may not be feeling the symptoms of stress.

HANDOUT: SQUEEZE OUT STRESS

If you feel stress, you are not alone. Far from it. Did you know that stress is one of the major issues facing us these days? It's true. A recent *Stress in America* survey conducted by the American Psychological Association found that 67% of persons reported suffering from a psychological symptom of stress the previous year. And yet, only about a third of those surveyed said they were doing a good job of managing stress.

You are going to use one of the easiest practices for reducing stress. If you haven't already done this, there are a couple of guidelines. First, don't wait for stress symptoms to reach a high level before using this technique. Start early. Secondly, practice often as a way of helping your body learn to relax—even when you don't think you need it.

Instructions:

- Find a quiet spot where you can sit or recline for up to five minutes. Sometimes it's helpful to find a place where there is low light or no light—especially if one of your stress symptoms is sensitivity to light.

- To begin, spend a few seconds pressing your heels into the floor or press your hands together if you are lying down. This is just to help you get grounded.

- Take three or four nice, satisfying, deep breaths. Exhale slowly. If you have learned how to do belly breathing, or diaphragmatic breathing, that is the kind of breathing that you will use here.

- Starting at the bottom of the body and moving upward, imagine squeezing all the tension into a ball with your feet as you inhale. Tense both feet (not to the point of pain) but just enough that you feel the tightness and tension. Hold this pose—also holding your in-breath—for a good five seconds, then release the ball of tension in your feet and exhale *sloooowwwlyyy* for as long as you can. Imagine that you have just squeezed out the stress and tension as your feet relax. Notice how nice it feels to let go of tightness in the feet. Now, inhale, imagining your breath traveling all the way down the body and settling into your feet. As you exhale, feel this part of the body relax even further.

- If you want, take a couple more long inhalations into the feet. With each slow exhalation you can feel the feet relax more and more deeply as any remaining tension or tightness is drained and squeezed out of the body. At this time, you can even smile inwardly at your feet, a part of the body that works hard carrying you around throughout the day.

- Next, you will move your attention up to the ankles, shins, and calves of both legs. Repeat the same squeezing out of the tension as you inhale and hold the tension before exhaling and releasing even more tension until nothing remains. Then, try smiling inwardly at this part of the body in gratitude.

- Little by little you will move up the entire body—tensing and squeezing each part into a ball to push out the stress as you also use your breath to do this. Move from the feet up to the knees, the thighs and hips, the stomach and abdominal area, the back muscles, the hands, the arms (forearm, elbow, upper arms), the neck and shoulders, and finally, the face, skull and scalp. If you are already experiencing pain in a part of the body, such as a headache, then don't tighten up that area as it may increase the pain or discomfort. Just skip over it.

- When you are done, let yourself revel in the deep peace and calm that pervades the body. Spend as long as you want to rest in this way. You may want to send your inner smile to the entire body at this time. Don't forget to send gratitude to yourself for taking care of your body and managing your stress.

Reflections: Congratulations on countering stress. How did it feel squeeze out stress in this way? How and when could you practice this so that you can keep stress from building up in the body?

_____

_____

_____

_____

_____

_____

_____

_____

_____

_____

Tool #34
Turning Down the Volume with Nature

THOUGHTS FOR THERAPISTS

Humans are extremely sensitive to sound. When you think about it, being surrounded by unwanted sound and noise pollution is much like walking into a room all jumbled and filled with clutter. Noise pollution can take many forms, such as the beeping of electronic devices, the humming of copy machines at the office, the vibration from air conditioning and heating systems, garbage trucks, and other street sounds. The rumble of cars rolling along freeways, for example, can travel for miles. Research has shown that noise can interrupt many areas of our lives. It can produce everything from sleep issues and impaired hearing to agitation and even stress-related cardiovascular symptoms.

Combining silence with the soothing quality of Nature connects us to something greater than ourselves. This quells the busy mind and lets us tap in to the wisdom within. Consider the words of botanist George Washington Carver, who developed hundreds of uses for peanut plants. Each day he would sit in wonder and silence with Nature, leading him to write:

> *Anything will give up its secrets if you love it enough.*
> *Not only have I found that when I talk to the little flower*
> *or to the little peanut they will give up their secrets,*
> *but I have found that when I silently commune with people*
> *they give up their secrets also—if you love them enough.*

Clients, too, can create new space, ideas, and perspectives from their situation by connecting with Nature and silence by using the following handout.

TIPS FOR WORKING WITH CLIENTS

- This handout and practice can work well in conjunction with Tool #15, *Sky Gazing with Nature*.

- Assess the level of noise in the environment where the client works and lives. How sensitive are they about sound, especially intrusive noise?

- In addition to sitting in Nature, help the client problem solve ways for reducing sound clutter on a daily basis.
  - There are noise-cancelling earphones that can be used to mask sound.
  - CDs with white noise or sounds of Nature are readily available.

HANDOUT: TURNING DOWN THE VOLUME WITH NATURE

If you are sensitive to sound and find intrusive sounds annoying and irritating, you are reacting normally to the stress produced by an increasingly noisy world. The fact that you are aware of sounds is the first step toward finding a remedy.

While we can't just snap our fingers and make that beeping (or "bleeping") garbage truck with noisy hydraulics disappear, we can take time to balance out and reduce the disorganizing and disturbing effects of unwanted noise.

This handout will offer some suggestions for finding calm and peace from stress by connecting with the soothing sounds of Nature and silence.

Let's start by reflecting on the words of Mahatma Gandhi. He wrote, "In the attitude of silence the soul finds the path in a clearer light, and what is elusive and deceptive resolves itself into crystal clearness." In this busy world no one will give us silence, but we can plant the seeds of silence ourselves.

Instructions:

1) <u>JUST LISTENING PRACTICE:</u> This is warm-up practice that you can use any time that sounds are annoying you. Here's how:

- Listen intently to the sounds around you right now. You are not trying to resist them or judge these sounds as good or bad. Whatever they are, just notice as many of them as you can. Sometimes, it is in resisting our experience that we get worn out and feel stress. Whenever you feel irritated or overwhelmed by sounds, try this non-judging, neutral method of noticing as many sounds as you can—without fighting them. (This is not to say you can't "turn down the volume" on these sounds, which you will learn to do next).

Reflections: How did it feel to focus your attention to sounds in this way, without judging them? What is it like to know you can choose to marvel at the sounds produced by modern technology? (Just as you can choose the *Just Listening Practice*, you can also choose the *Turning Down the Volume with Nature* practice!)

_____

_____

_____

_____

_____

_____

_____

_____

2) <u>TURNING DOWN THE VOLUME WITH NATURE PRACTICE:</u> Since Nature can be soothing, we are going to bring Nature and silence together.

- Find a natural spot as far from the mechanical world as you can. This might be a park, the backyard, wherever you can find Nature. You don't need to get out in the woods or up on a mountaintop to turn down the volume!

- If possible, find a quiet place to sit. (You can sit, stand, or walk with this practice). Now, widen your gaze. Let all of this natural world seep in. Next, let your eyes gently be drawn to whatever natural feature attracts it. This might be a flower, a tree, a patch of grass, the chirping of a bird, a scurrying squirrel, the broad blue sky or clouds floating high above.
- Focus in on this aspect of Nature that you are drawn toward. Don't analyze, just experience it. Lose yourself in it. If you have worries, imagine casting them outward, letting Nature, which is so big and immense, hold your worries for you.
- Let yourself sit in the peace, wonder, and magnificent mystery of Nature. Focus in on its sounds. Experience deeply how different these are from the sounds of your normal day. Go deeper as you continue to peer into the Nature around you. Let yourself notice all the tiniest details, the uniqueness of each tree branch and cloud as you immerse yourself in the outdoors.
- Don't be afraid to go beyond. Beyond word and thought into the formless, the spacious. Rest in this sublime place for as long as you need.
- Sometimes Nature may speak to you, wordlessly, of course. It may help you tap into your own wisdom or help you find some clarity around a problem. Don't force this. But don't be surprised if Nature's silence comes to your aid in this way.
- Conclude your *Turning Down the Volume with Nature* practice with a centering statement, blessing, or gratitude.

Reflections: Can you think of one small way this practice was beneficial? How could you use this during the day? Is there a way to experience this even indoors?

_____

_____

_____

_____

_____

_____

There are other ways to turn down the volume, or at least counteract sound pollution and noise clutter. These include noise cancelling earphones or CDs that feature the soothing sounds found in the natural world, such as mild drizzling rain, rumbling ocean waves, or the soft song of the forest. Which of these methods—or others that you can think of—would help you to turn down the volume when you can't easily step out into Nature?

_____

_____

_____

_____

_____

_____

_____

Tool #35
Take a Stress Pause

THOUGHTS FOR THERAPISTS

In our non-stop high speed, hi-tech world, we are bombarded daily by hundreds, if not thousands, of emails, tweets, advertisements, text messages and Internet pop-up windows. The effect of speed, working across multiple time zones, and porous boundaries between work and home are setting the stage for unprecedented levels of stress.

The ability to pause is a simple act that can allow us to return to the present, to come back to our "senses" so to speak. At another level, slowing down to pay attention in this way accesses the prefrontal cortex, the regulatory part of the human brain. This is required if we are to pause and reflect on the many possibilities awaiting us, rather than just impulsively jumping in without thinking.

Author and philosopher Huston Smith once said, "I have a slow mind, but it's a good mind." So, too, can we embrace slowness as a way to enter that vast reflective space that lies within. This allows us to process and make connections with the whole of our vast life experience. This is known as wisdom, and slowing down helps us access it.

TIPS FOR WORKING WITH CLIENTS

- The *Take a Stress Pause* practice can be bundled very nicely with these two tools as a way of slowing down a hectic pace and finding peace:
  - Tool #11, *The Power of Breath*
  - Tool #16, *BE-THIS. Sense Grounding.*
- This practice can be done anywhere, and it can be useful as a centering practice before entering a moment of uncertainty or transition when moving between two places, or environments.

HANDOUT: TAKE A STRESS PAUSE

Are things speeding up in your life? Do you feel like you just don't have a moment to take a breather? Are you feeling overwhelmed, over-stimulated, and pressured to make too many decisions too fast?

Fortunately, this easy exercise is an ideal way to create a buffer from speed and stress and to slow things down a bit. If you're stressed and reactive, and feel that you would benefit by stepping back, this could be just the way to open a new doorway. In addition, you can take a stress pause anytime you feel stuck in an old habit or routine.

Instructions:

Use the acronym S-T-O-P to take a pause anytime, anywhere. Simply state each letter and then follow along with what it means. "STOP" doesn't mean to stop everything, but rather, to be more present, aware, at ease, and in flow with what is happening all around you. From this centered, flexible, and aware place, you don't have to react out of fear or impulse. You can be more available in order to make better choices and observe all the options and possibilities before you.

S-*Stand*: Slow the pace by standing in place and taking two or three nice, calming, deep belly breaths. By doing this you are making a conscious and purposeful decision to slow things down. You are deciding to be in control, rather than let external pressures trigger you to reaction and stress.

T-*Tune-In*: In this moment, tune-in to your body with full presence. Feel yourself grounded and connected to the earth, just like a favorite tree. Slowly scan the body starting from the tips of the toes and moving up to the top of the head. As you move upwards, be aware of where you may be holding onto tension or negative emotions. Breathe into the tension and let it go.

Optionally, you can visualize breathing a soothing white or golden light into that tension-filled area. Then as you exhale, imagine your breath carrying the tension down the body—finally releasing it through the bottom of the feet. Take as many breaths as needed to release tension and negativity.

O-*Observe*: Change the channel by closely observing your external environment. Focus on the surroundings, taking note of at least three unique or pleasant things—colors, shapes, objects, sounds, or textures that you like. If you are in a familiar environment, look for even the smallest detail you may not have noticed before—like the space between the wood grains on the table, or the different shades of color in the carpet. Just immerse and ground yourself in your surroundings like this for a minute or two as you find something that delights or surprises you.

P-*Possibility*: Pause to reflect on the openness, spaciousness, and possibilities that lie before you. You have just gone off auto-pilot and are now free to choose a new and beneficial direction. If you had been feeling reactive or angry, for example, you can look with fresh eyes at the variety of different choices and options before you. Who says that right now you couldn't sing, smile, call a supportive friend, take a nice walk, or get a scoop of your favorite ice cream? You might even just feel pleased that you have completed this exercise. Stretch your mind and see how far it can go!

Reflections: What was it like for you to S-T-O-P in this way? What did you notice most?

_____

_____

_____

What kinds of new possibilities could this practice help you to find? How could you get creative with using this practice?

_____

_____

_____

_____

_____

Tool #36
"Breathing Into" Stress Detox

THOUGHTS FOR THERAPISTS

Stress and tension can build up quickly in the body. In workshops, I have found that a body awareness practice is a good way to discharge this tension, as well as help individuals notice how the body acts as an early warning system that informs us of stress build-up.

The practice of "breathing into" is a visualization practice. Some doctors think that placing one's awareness on a part of the body mobilizes white blood cells and instantly directs them to the site. If this does indeed occur, it may provide a clue as to why many people find this practice helpful in discharging general pain, headaches, tightness, and discomfort.

What's important is that this practice can get clients connected to the body and encourages them to them use deep breathing in order to better regulate the parasympathetic nervous system and buffer the body from stress.

TIPS FOR WORKING WITH CLIENTS

- Any breathing practice, such as the *Breathing Into Stress Detox*, will benefit from first teaching Tool #11, *The Power of Breath*.
  - Tool #33, *Squeeze Out Stress*, is also ideal for releasing tension and can be used in conjunction with the *Breathing Into Stress Detox*.
- Make sure clients are okay with visualization before engaging them in this practice.
  - Clients may have a particular color, sound, or image that helps them visualize. Use whatever form of visualization works best for them.

HANDOUT: "BREATHING INTO" STRESS DETOX

The *Breathing Into Stress Detox* practice is about bringing your body back into balance, and as such its purpose is to help discharge and release tension and stress that builds up in the body. (This practice is not intended as a substitute for getting proper medical care for even a moderate, serious, or persistent condition).

That is not to minimize this practice, because coming into balance and harmony is critical for daily functioning and entering the moment with full presence. Even a mild headache could be a sign of being out of balance that disrupts your ability to focus and savor the moment.

For practice, you will use your imagination to visualize that you could breathe past the lungs and into any part of the body.

Instructions:

This is a simple practice once you get the hang of it. Find a nice quiet place where you can sit or lie down. You can do this for up to five minutes or longer if you want.

- Close your eyes and bring awareness to the body. Notice where you feel tightness, tension, or even pain.
- Once you've located the place where you want to relieve tension, you will take in a long breath. As you inhale, imagine a healing or soothing white or golden light coming in through the crown of your head— you could just see this light coming in with your breath through the normal breathing pathways. Picture this light traveling to the location where you are experiencing tightness or tension.
- Let the soothing light fill up the affected area. Let it seep all the way down to the cells of that part of the body.
- Take a long, slow exhalation. As you do this, visualize your breath carrying any tightness, tension, and any impurities down the body. The breath carries these impurities down the legs and finally, out of the bottom of your feet—where they are deposited harmlessly back into the Earth for recycling (or composting).
- Repeat the above process as many times as necessary until the tightness or tension is reduced or all remaining impurities are drained away. Optionally, you can add the following healing or balancing intention: "May this part of my body attain full balance and harmony as it is intended to be."

Reflections: Write in the space below your experience of the *Breathing Into Stress Detox*. What changes, if any, in your body tension did you notice?

_____

_____

_____

The idea of visualizing a healing white or golden light are just suggestions. Are there other colors or imagery (such as flowing water), or sounds that you would find helpful when doing this practice?

_____

_____

_____

_____

Tool #37
Warm Hands Visualization

LEARNING STYLES

The following learning styles are compatible with this practice:

Visual-Spatial

Bodily-Kinesthetic-Tactile

THOUGHTS FOR THERAPISTS

In *Anatomy of an Illness*, mind-body pioneer Norman Cousins wrote, "The regenerative and restorative force in human beings is at the core of human uniqueness." When dealing with stress, this powerful restorative capability can be tapped through the *Warm Hands Visualization*. Hand-warming through mental awareness is a biofeedback technique that was extensively researched and used at the Menninger Clinic in Kansas. Researchers found that by raising the temperature in their hands, patients suffering from headaches were able to significantly lessen the severity of their symptoms.

We now understand that bringing blood to the extremities—the hands and feet—actually quiets down the sympathetic nervous system—the body's flight, flight, and freeze response. Instead of stress hormones being released into the body and causing blood vessel constriction and muscle contraction, these are relaxed and unclenched, allowing for improved blood flow and lowering blood pressure. The body's arousal level is now being controlled and monitored by the individual using this practice. This not only calms the body, but it gives the practitioner an improved sense of efficacy and self-control. It's a win-win.

Best of all, the *Warm Hands Visualization* practice is portable and can be used anywhere as a method of producing a calm state of mind—even in the face of life's daily stresses, challenges, and hassles.

TIPS FOR WORKING WITH CLIENTS

- Use the handout that follows as a readable script for guiding clients through the *Warm Hands Visualization* for the first time. After, clients can refer to the handout, or you may want to record the script for them.
- Consider getting a stress thermometer or stress meter (there are many different kinds available) that can be taped onto the tip of a client's finger. This provides solid evidence of how they are literally raising the temperature in their hands after practicing the *Warm Hands Visualization*.

- Like any skill, deep relaxation practices can take time to learn. So if the client doesn't see immediate results—find out where and when they are practicing—which can affect the outcome.
  - Ideally, it's best to practice when quiet and undisturbed.
  - Lying down can be helpful, but sitting is okay.
  - Having enough time and not feeling time-pressured is important.
  - Encourage the client to continue practicing.
- Consider teaching the *Warm Hands Visualization* in tandem with the progressive body relaxation practice, Tool #33, *Squeeze Out Stress*. This will provide clients with two very different, but effective, tools for de-stressing.

HANDOUT: WARM HANDS VISUALIZATION

The Power of Bio-Feedback

Have you ever tried or heard of bio-feedback? It has a long history and has been found to be very effective for reducing stress, turning down the body's stress system, and for turning *on* the body's relaxation system. Relaxation techniques like this one have been successfully implemented and used in medical clinics around the country to lower blood pressure, lessen headaches, improve sleep, and other stress-related conditions.

In this visualization, you will imagine warming up your hands and feet. By doing this, you move blood toward the body's extremities. This has been shown to help blood vessels and muscles relax. Body temperature on the surface of the hands is around 75 degrees. Research has shown that many people can increase the temperature in their hands by as much as 10 degrees. In fact, to show you that this works, before starting, you can tape a thermometer or stress device to the tip of your middle or ring finger. Notice the reading on the thermometer. After your visualization, you can read the thermometer again and see how much the temperature has changed. By doing this practice, you are actually controlling your autonomic nervous system, regulating it and bringing your body into greater balance. Now, let's begin. Follow along with the steps below.

1) **Practice this somewhere that is quiet and where you will not be disturbed for the next 10 minutes.** It may also be helpful to lie down when practicing this visualization, although it's okay to sit. You will close your eyes in order visualize this in as much detail as possible. You can even state the mental intention for this exercise as follows: "My intention right now is to relax my body and reduce stress and invite a state of peace, balance, and calm."

2) **Start by taking some nice long, slow breaths.** If you have learned belly breathing, you can do that. When you are comfortably settled in, you will picture yourself in front of an elevator that will carry you down several floors to the beach.

3) **The elevator door opens, and you step in. Press the button on the car that will take you down five floors to the beach.** The elevator has a big window that lets you look out on the beach. It is a bright, sunny day without a cloud in the sky. The palm trees (or any trees you want to imagine) are blowing in a gentle breeze.

   As the elevators moves down past each floor, you can hear the calming voice from the elevator that counts down each floor. "Floor Four . . ." "Floor Three" intones the voice. As you move down past each floor you can feel yourself getting more and more relaxed. "Floor Two," you hear the voice say. Now you are feeling much calmer, as if all your tension is leaving the body in anticipation of your visit to the beach. You feel the elevator slow down as you approach the beach level. "Floor One . . . Welcome to the Beach," says the warm voice. The doors open and you step onto a sandy path leading to the beach. You can picture yourself removing your shoes and feeling the warmth of the sand envelop your feet as you follow the path toward the expansive beach.

4) **You carry with you a large beach blanket. When you get closer to the clear, aqua colored water, find a place to spread your blanket.** You can picture yourself lying down with your clothes on, or you may be wearing a swimsuit or shorts and a top. Notice how it feels to let your body spread out on the blanket. Feel the support of the warm sand beneath you. As you lie down, you notice how the heat of the sun warms your hands. Notice your hands as they start to soak in all the warmth and heat. Let them soak it in, feeling them warm up under the hot sun. In fact, picture yourself moving your hands onto the sand. The heat of the sand is hot, but not uncomfortably so, and it warms your hands even more.

5) **Notice all your senses at the beach.** Pause for a minute to notice the sounds of the water and the waves. The rhythmic sound is comforting to hear. You may hear the seagulls flapping their wings or chirping a melodic song. At the same time, notice the smell of the beach, the ocean, and maybe even the scent of sun tanning

lotion that wafts through the air. Feel the sand on your hands, as well as your back and legs touching the warm blanket. Now, focus on your feet. Notice how they, too, have been warming up. You may visualize putting them on the sand, too. The pulsing of the sun's rays are beating down on your feet and your hands, heating them up more each second. Notice how nice it feels to have that warm sensation in your hands and feet. Notice how the heat extends from the top of the hand down to the palm, and all the way out to the fingers and fingertips.

6) **Relish and immerse yourself in the warmth of the sun, the sand, and the beach.** Your hands are heating up even more now, as the sun's rays continue to heat them from above while the hot sand heats them from below. Feel the warmness building even more. Know that it is okay to sit like this. There is nothing more important to attend to right now. You are giving yourself this break at the beach, because you enjoy the feeling of warmth and peace that it gives you. Continue to let your hands and feet get warmer and warmer. When they have reached maximum warmness, you can set the intention to stand and return to the elevator.

7) **You might want to brush off the sand first! Now, picture yourself walking back up the sandy path to the elevator.** Stepping on, you feel all warm and relaxed. When the door closes, you can see yourself pressing the top button, which is Floor Five. As the soothing elevator voice announces each floor on the way up, you can feel yourself getting more alert and filled with a complete sense of well-being. "Floor Two . . . Floor Three" says the voice as you feel a sense of inner balance and peace. At "Floor Four" you are reminded that you can use this special elevator anytime you want to go down five floors to the beach and savor the welcoming warmth that waits for you.

8) **As the elevator slows to a stop, the calming voice announces, "Floor Five, thank you for coming to your special beach. Please come visit us again!"** The door opens wide and, as you get step off the elevator, you feel completely at ease, energized, refocused and ready to greet your day. Open your eyes at this point with a nice, long inhale and exhale.

Reflections: If you have taped a thermometer to your finger, look at its reading. Did it change? By how much?

_____
_____
_____
_____

What does this practice say about your ability to use your mind to affect your body? Also, the idea of visualizing a beach is just one way of imagining your hands and feet heating up.

_____
_____
_____
_____

How could you make this a practice that you use on a regular basis? What would that look like? How would that be helpful to you in regulating stress?

_____
_____
_____
_____

Tool #38
Share an Uplifting and Hopeful Story

LEARNING STYLES

The following learning styles are compatible with this practice:

Verbal-Linguistic

Musical-Sound

Social-Interpersonal

Existential-Meaning

THOUGHTS FOR THERAPISTS

Our very thoughts can create a metaphorical train (of thoughts) that carries us to places we'd be better off not visiting! The metaphor of a train provides a useful perspective and visual metaphor. I still remember the time I asked a ruminating client this question: *If you step onto the train of negative, ruminating thoughts, where does it take you? What is at the end of the line?* His answer was direct and to the point: *It takes me to Dwellsville.* Although we laughed in that moment, the implications of his statement were profound. I've heard many other answers through the years, such as *Anxietyland* and *Stressville.* Fortunately, there are many ways to get off the stress train and step back onto the platform. And, if someone gets on the train, they can always get off at the next stop—so they don't have to go all the way to the end of the line.

Just as a negative or stressful story can buy a ticket to the stress train, an uplifting story can purchase a ticket to an entirely different train and experience of hope. Psychologist C. R. Snyder was one of the foremost researchers in the field of hope. He found that those who were low in hope had difficulty finding resources. Since not having supportive resources is one cause of stress, sharing or telling an uplifting story helps to create relationships. More importantly, it contains the potential for motivating and teaching how to overcome obstacles and get help from others—the seeds of hope.

TIPS FOR WORKING WITH CLIENTS

- *Share an Uplifting and Hopeful Story* matches up well with Tool #26, *Savoring Success—Past, Present, and Future.* Consider using these two practices jointly.
- This practice is good for clients who may be stuck on the stress train and don't know it. The *Share an Uplifting and Hopeful Story* can get them unstuck and more aware of the stories they are telling.

- Hope is a learned skill that can be modeled through storytelling.
  - This is an important interpersonal practice that can be effective in groups as well as for individuals. In groups, uplifting stories of hope can be told to the entire group, brought in as assignments, or shared partner to partner.
- Some useful resources for hope include C.R. Snyder's *The Handbook of Hope* and *The Psychology of Hope*. For children and hope, try *Hope for the Journey: Helping Children Through Good Times and Bad* by Snyder, McDermott, Cook, and Rapoff. (see: **Bibliography/Resources**)

HANDOUT: SHARE AN UPLIFTING AND HOPEFUL STORY

The stories we tell can create stress, and they can relieve stress. Stories can also help us find hope and the resources that can provide motivating support, as well as vital information for overcoming obstacles that are in the way.

Let's start with some quotes about how our perceptions and stories affect us.

I'm an old man and have known a great many troubles in my life—most of which never happened.

—Mark Twain

Hope is an orientation of the spirit, an orientation of the heart. Hope is not the conviction that something will turn out well, but the certainty that something makes sense regardless of how it turns out.

—Vaclav Havel

Spring is hidden in all seasons.

—Zen Master Daiensai

For this practice, you will see how an uplifting and hopeful story can reduce stress or even help to build relationships with others by hearing such a story. Follow along with these steps to find an uplifting story of hope from your own life. To qualify as an uplifting story, it needs the following attributes:

- The story needs to present a challenge that you faced. It needs to have "lows" and "highs" like any good, compelling story!
- It needs to end with a "high" or have been resolved positively or beneficially. (Even acceptance can be a positive outcome).
- Others must have helped you to some degree in reaching resolution, such as:
  - Offering advice that got you thinking of new ways to reach your goal
  - Giving you useful information
  - Inspiring or motivating you to move forward

1) In the space below you will write about your story in detail. (Optionally, at another time you can share this story with another). Make sure that you include the following items in order to describe the entire story:
- Who/What/Why/Where/When/How: Like a news reporter just stating the facts, describe when this story occurred in your life. How did this situation come about? Who else was involved in this story/situation? (You can always change names to keep this confidential).

_____

_____

_____

_____

_____

_____

- Describe the negative feelings you were dealing with of being stuck. In other words, what was like for you emotionally to face the challenge of this story? Tell all the feelings—whether sadness, hopelessness, frustration, anger, etc.— that you experienced. (These are the lows).

  _____

  _____

  _____

  _____

  _____

- Once again, like a journalist, describe the facts about how you found a supportive resource, got help or assistance, or sought out useful advice that helped move you forward to find resolution and a positive outcome. This part of the story tells of your own resourcefulness and ability to connect with others in a trusting and positive way. (A resource could be a historical person that you admire for how they overcame obstacles, or even wise, strong, unwavering characters from your favorite story or film).

  _____

  _____

  _____

  _____

  _____

- Finally, write down the positive emotions you felt upon moving forward and getting unstuck. Tell all the feelings—whether lightness, hope, happiness, tears of joy, relief, etc.— that you experienced. (These are the highs).

  _____

  _____

  _____

  _____

  _____

Reflections: Sometimes it's easy to forget all the details of our own uplifting stories. What was it like to journal an uplifting story of hope from your life in this way?

_____

_____

_____

_____

How did it make you feel to re-experience the highs? What did you learn most about yourself and your strengths by writing down this story?

_____

_____

_____

_____

What would it be like for you to share an uplifting story with others—as well as to hear another's uplifting story?

_____

_____

_____

Seek out uplifting stories this week wherever you can, noting them in the space below. You might even consider keeping a journal of hopeful stories. See what they have in common, notice how connecting with others often turns challenging stories into positive and uplifting ones.

_____

_____

_____

_____

Tool #39
Be the Pebble

THOUGHTS FOR THERAPISTS

Stress can create conditions in the mind that are as unpredictable and turbulent as a roiling sea. Used properly and in conjunction with a word or phrase, the mind can find quiet beneath those waves. In *Calming Your Anxious Mind*, stress reduction expert Dr. Jeffrey Brantley writes, "One of the oldest and most common meditation practices to build concentration and mindfulness focuses on the breath itself [and] practicing awareness of breathing immediately brings you back to the present moment. With the breath as your focus, the natural ability of the mind and body to calm can arise."

The *Be the Pebble* practice introduced here will blend breathing with a calming word or phrase that will act as a metaphorical pebble. This "pebble" thought will drop anyone below the surface of stress and chaos, and let the mind come to rest—like any pebble does—on the bottom of the ocean or river floor. After all, what more does a pebble need to do than just 'be' a pebble?

The calming nature of this practice has long been used for stress, and has even been found to quell anxiety in students and improve the ability to focus and concentrate. That should come as no surprise, since this practice places attention on the calming word(s) and then sustains attention on it. With attention-splintering technology like Twitter and endless text messaging, this practice is a useful tool for attending to this moment, while calming the mind and paying attention now . . . and now . . . and yes, now!

TIPS FOR WORKING WITH CLIENTS

- Use the instructions below as a readable script to guide clients through this for the first time when in session. Other meditative and contemplative practices that match up with this one include the following:
  - Tool #47, *Lessons from Nature*
  - Tool #48, *Loving-Kindness Affirmation*

- *Be the Pebble* practice is not confined to being a verbal practice. Some clients, in particular those with ADD, may find that it easier to focus on an image over and over, rather than a word.
- For clients who are more tactile and movement oriented, the pebble word can be stated along with movement, such as taking a step or even lifting a weight.
  - Start with the regular practice and then adapt it as needed for clients.
  - This practice works best when used on a regular, scheduled basis—such as five or 10 minutes a day or every other day.

Handout: Be the Pebble

A Practice to Quiet and Calm the Mind

Sometimes, stress can get our minds so active and 'wound up' that they are like a choppy ocean. If you've ever gone out to sea on waters like that, you know that getting seasick is no fun. For many, having a mind that is as choppy and turbulent as that water can have very much the same effect.

But what if you were a pebble that could drop below the surface of that tumultuous water and get down to where the water was still, calm, and peaceful? The pebble wouldn't be experiencing the chaos up above. It would just be at rest, peaceful and snug on the bottom of the ocean floor. That's just what this practice can help you do when you're stressed and spinning with thoughts.

For this practice, you are going to use a word or a phrase that will serve as your "pebble" that can focus your mind and help you drop below the surface of those noisy, riotous waves. This is a gentle practice that guides you to that place of greater peace and inner hospitality. Follow along with the three steps below.

Instructions:

1) Choose a Word or Phrase

To begin, you'll want to choose a word or short phrase that you can focus on and repeat in your mind, over and over. The words or phrases you can use for this practice are infinite. You could, for example, mentally repeat words such as "one," "quiet mind," "peace," "shalom," or "now." I have found that many people like to use the word "pebble" because it is neutral and has no associations for them. You might even decide to use a prayer, such as the ancient Jesus Prayer: "Lord Jesus Christ, have mercy upon me." Feel free to get creative and use words that feel good. For example, I know an avid golfer who finds the phrase "bogey-free" to be calming and helpful for him. If the word you are using doesn't feel right, you can always try another one next time.

It's also a good idea to avoid words that associate you with a particular memory. If you find that a word stimulates memory or intrudes by creating more thoughts, you can choose a more neutral word. Even using a neutral word like "one" has been shown to lower stress.

The purpose of this practice is to release stress and gently quiet your mind by turning it away from the turbulence. You can think of this practice as dropping a pebble into rushing water. The word you focus on will gently take you beneath the choppy surface to where there are no waves; your mind and thoughts will settle down and grow quiet in the stillness beneath the waves. You can also imagine this practice as a way of calming the surface so you can float on top of the still water.

Once you begin to focus on the word, allow yourself at least 10 minutes of quiet time to reflect on your word or phrase. It helps to find a quiet place to sit, either indoors or outside. While you can do this practice lying down, it's better to sit up, because it will be easier to stay awake. This is true even if you are sitting up in bed. Avoid practicing for at least one hour after a meal, because you may get too drowsy to stay focused.

2) Sit Quietly With Eyes Closed

Now, sitting quietly, close your eyes. While repeating your word, you will be placing about 10-15% of your awareness on the breath. Make sure you breathe evenly, and into the belly. As you think of your word, do not concentrate hard; this is not about forcing or creating too much effort. This is a gentle and effortless way of resting in the stillness beneath the water. Imagine that you are just *preferring or favoring* your chosen word over other thoughts. If your mind wanders off into thinking about the past or the future for a while, that's okay. Even if you get drowsy, that's okay, too. Just gently return to your word again.

Sometimes, it may feel like your word has gone inward, as if it's still there even though you're not repeating it. If this happens, simply allow yourself to experience it this way. Your other senses may also intrude as you repeat your word. You may hear a noise or you may feel a sensation in your body. Don't push these away; rather, just notice them and return to the breath and the word.

3) Allow Negative Feelings To Pass

Sometimes, strong feelings or emotions may occur while you are repeating your word. If you experience a strong negative feeling, see what it is like to sit with it until it passes. Your mind will naturally be drawn to it, and you don't need to explain or understand it, but let yourself notice if it increases or lessens in intensity. If for any reason it doesn't dissolve away and you get uncomfortable, you can always stop the practice by opening your eyes, distracting yourself, or just resting. Know that you can always return to this practice later.

At other times, you may experience an uplifting feeling while doing this practice. Whatever your experience may be today, the next practice session may bring totally different feelings. Give yourself permission to be open to whatever arises.

I like to think of this as a gentle practice, so if you feel the need to shift your position on the ground or chair or bed, go ahead and do so—but do so with full awareness. You may want to use a watch or clock the first few times you try this. After a while, you will sense when your 10 minutes are up. Before you open your eyes, allow yourself to just sit in the presence of your body with compassion. Then, slowly open your eyes. You may also want to end your 10 minutes of attentiveness with a short message or blessing of thanks.

Reflections: How did this practice settle your mind? Were you able to stay with your pebble word(s) in an easy way, as a preference, and not have to force it?

_____

_____

_____

_____

_____

Try keeping track of how long you practice, such as from five to 10 minutes, for example. Make note of your stress or anxiety level before and after you do practice *Be the Pebble*. Use a 1-10 scale, where 10 is the highest level and 1 is the lowest. This way, you may learn what amount of time is optimal for you.

_____

_____

_____

_____

As with any other practice, this one works best when used regularly. How could you schedule this? What times of day do you think it would be most effective or helpful to reduce stress?

_____

_____

_____

_____

Tool #40
Be a Smart Stress-Avoider

THOUGHTS FOR THERAPISTS

Learning how to detox the body from stress by using the various mind-body practices in Section 4 of *The Mindfulness Toolbox* is an important step. But often it's easy to forget about one of the key aspects of stress: How to avoid it in the first place!

Psychologist, researcher and author, Robert Epstein, has developed a grid of four stress competency areas when he tests people for their stress reduction capabilities. It makes good sense that each of these areas needs to be addressed in order to deal effectively with stress. These four areas include how well a person 1) manages sources of stress, 2) prevents stress from occurring, 3) practices relaxation techniques, and 4) manages thoughts.

While learning stress reduction techniques is a useful tool, why not try to manage and avoid the stress that is right in front of us? This *Be a Smart Stress Avoider* handout will look at those areas where we can be proactive in preventing stress.

TIPS FOR WORKING WITH CLIENTS

- After identifying stressors, help clients problem solve ways they can avoid them.
- If desired, you can work through the worksheet with your client, or have them bring it back after working with it at home.
  - It can be helpful to problem-solve the "manageable" and "avoidable" section of the handout with the client.
- Here are two web-based resources that offer short online tests that can be given to clients in order to measure their stress levels.
  - The Perceived Stress Scale (PSS), a 10-question inventory developed by psychologist Sheldon Cohen (mindgarden.com).
  - The Epstein Stress-Management Inventory for Individuals (ESMI-i), a 28-question inventory (mystressmanagementskills.com).

HANDOUT: BE A SMART STRESS AVOIDER

Right now, think about one thing that gets you stressed out. Is it the traffic in the morning going to work? The chores you face at home? The stack of messy mail and bills that you haven't yet gotten cleaned up and paid? It's normal that there seem to be things we just can't control that drive up our stress levels. Or, can we control them—even a little? While it's a great idea to use relaxation methods to de-stress, it also makes a lot of sense to manage and avoid stress when and where we can.

1) Take a look at what stress in your life is manageable or preventable. Here is a list of 60 potential stressors. To begin, circle the ones that are significant sources of stress

2) Write the stresses that you circled in the table below, in the left column, "Sources of Stress."

SOURCES OF STRESS

driving	rush hour traffic	health
deadlines	unopened mail	chores
clutter	relationships	loud noises
bright lights	weather	other drivers
animals/wild animals	repairs/car repairs	bad smells
air pollution/congestion	fears	credit card bills
politics	religion	retirement (saving for)
unemployment	divorce/going to court	underemployment
crying children	children's safety	bosses
running late	running behind at work	co-workers
crime	personal safety	finances
health insurance	aging	medical/dental expenses
diet/weight	studying/homework	staying up w/technology
tech overload (email/texting)	planning/making meals	school exams
homework	entertaining/visitors	holidays
goals	procrastination	parenting
natural disasters	death/grief	moving/packing
starting a new job	planning a wedding	changing schools
missing work	work trainings	work reviews
grocery shopping	an addiction	public speaking

3) In the middle column, rate your significant stressors on a 1-10 scale, where 1 is low and 10 is the highest level of stress.

4) In the right column, write an "M" if the stress is manageable, and "A" if it is avoidable. An avoidable stress might be rush hour traffic, which could be avoided by taking a new route or scheduling appointments before or after the rush hour, if possible. Rush hour traffic might also be manageable by leaving for work a few minutes earlier.

Get as creative as you can about managing or avoiding stress. For example, if you have too many papers and bills cluttering up your dining room table, you might manage this stress by getting a new chest of drawers or a file cabinet to hold and organize these items. Write your management or avoidance strategy in the right hand column.

Sources of Stress	Stress Level 1-10	Manageable/Avoidable

Reflections: How do you think your methods for avoiding or managing stress will affect your ratings? Write your predictions below, and then you can see how accurate they are when you implement your ideas.

_____

_____

_____

What will be the biggest challenge you will face in implementing any of your stress reduction plans? Which plan(s) will be the easiest to apply?

_____

_____

_____

Since it may not always be possible to completely avoid stress, what stress relaxation practices could you employ? Which stressors can you use these with?

_____

_____

_____

Consider problem-solving with others to see if there are other ways to work with the stressors you are facing. Write down the names of those who can help you problem-solve. Also, is there someone in your life who is willing to lessen your stress load by handling one of your stresses? As you work to dwindle the sources of stress in your life, you may find a greater sense of ease and a brighter, lighter attitude!

_____

_____

Section 5

MINDFULNESS TOOLS FOR PAIN

Tool #41
Surf the Body (The Body Scan)

THOUGHTS FOR THERAPISTS

Pain is a major daily stressor. A stress survey conducted by the American Psychological Association found that 69% of respondents—almost seven out of 10—complained of a physical symptom related to stress. In addition, there are countless more experiencing chronic pain conditions, from irritable bowel syndrome and chronic fatigue syndrome to back pain and other forms of inflammation. Rather than use addictive pain relievers with significant negative side effects, many would prefer a more natural alternative.

The *Surf the Body* handout here is not a replacement for medication, but might assist the patient to better tolerate and manage pain—and, in some cases, help reduce the level of prescription pain relievers. There is solid evidence for using this practice. For example, the research study, "Brain mechanisms supporting the modulation of pain by mindfulness meditation," published in *The Journal of Neuroscience*, described how mindfulness meditation reduced pain unpleasantness by 57% and reduced pain intensity by 40%.

The key benefits of *Surf the Body* practice are twofold. First, it changes the way in which someone experiences pain sensations in the body. It can help an individual learn to distinguish between the actual *sensation* and the *story* of that sensation. As an example, one who has lost a career because of a painful condition may have the devastating loss of that career triggered by the sensation of pain. The body scan helps separate the two. Yes, the sensation and the pain are related, but they are very different and distinct from one another. This awareness can help individuals deal with the sensation instead of adding on the optional suffering that comes from the story of loss.

Secondly, the body scan teaches someone how to train the mind to pay attention in a particular way—like a neutral, impassive witness. Thus, one experiences pain sensations in a new way. It also helps teach how to focus and sustain attention, instead of having the mind wander off like an energetic puppy dog. *Surf the Body* is a good practice for training the puppy dog mind.

TIPS FOR WORKING WITH CLIENTS

- If you are going to work with clients using the body scan practice, it is advisable that you first have your own *Surf the Body* practice. This will help you prepare for the questions that may arise.
  - For clients experiencing anxiety, consider using *Surf the Body* in tandem with Tool #17, *Sensing and Rating Anxiety in the Body*.

- Use the instructions in the handout as a readable script for guiding clients through the body scan in session. This can be recorded, and there are online and CD recordings of the body scan, a.k.a. the Inner Smile Meditation available.

- Always let clients know that they can stop or take a time-out at any time.
  - This is important if someone has body trauma or is dissociated from the body—such as those with eating disorder conditions like anorexia and bulimia.
  - For those with body trauma or dissociation, a limited form of the body scan, such as just scanning the pinky finger, can introduce this to someone in a more innocuous and safer way.

- The body scan can be helpful not just for those experiencing pain, but for many conditions where getting grounded in the body can be helpful—from substance use recovery to anxiety and depression.

HANDOUT: SURF THE BODY (THE BODY SCAN)

Find a quiet place where you can sit or lie down for several minutes as you follow along with the steps outlined below. **Please Note**—If you suffer from trauma or experience severe discomfort that you feel you can't tolerate while surfing the body, you can always open your eyes and stop. You are always in control whenever you do this practice.

Instructions:

Here are some orienting thoughts before starting. You will be placing your attention on your body. The purpose of this activity is not to relax, but to increase your awareness and notice any body sensations that may be present from moment to moment. If you feel discomfort at any time, you can remind yourself that this is simply a sensation. The sensation does not define who you are. You are simply observing signals, and you may notice that the awareness of sensation of pain is not the sensation or pain itself, but just awareness. This may lead to greater understanding about discomfort or pain.

If at any time any sensation feels overwhelming, you can open your eyes and stop, or move to another body part where there is no pain or negative feeling. Know, however, that by resting with the discomfort, you are allowing yourself to bear witness to the feeling and sensation that exists, and experiencing the fullness of what is occurring. If you have pain in a certain area of the body—such as your neck or shoulders—you may find that focusing on that area increases the sensation. Again, you can always move focus to another part of the body and return to the painful area later.

Remember that this practice may or may not produce relaxation. It will be different each time you practice it. You are encouraged to let go of expectations as part of this practice. This is a very proactive process by which you are actually scanning the motor and sensory cortex of your brain. It's kind of like massaging the brain and body from the inside out.

1) **To begin, center your mind on your body's presence.** Take three deep breaths and feel your diaphragm move. Feel how marvelous it is that each breath fills your lungs, sends oxygen to your muscles and organs, and sustains you. You may want to wiggle your toes and feel how effortlessly they follow your command. Take a few moments to feel grateful for this body, this extraordinary gift that you possess.

2) **You are going to use your imagination with the practice.** Let's imagine, for example, that your breath could carry your awareness into any part of the body. Let's try now, by taking that first breath. Picture the breath going down the left side of the body and bringing your awareness with it. Bring the breath down the left leg and into the left foot and all way out to your toes. Let your full awareness settle into the toes. Just notice whatever sensations are rising and falling. If there's no sensation, that's okay too. You don't need to create one.

   As you do this, you can spend a moment to acknowledge how your toes have been masterfully constructed to help you walk and carry your weight. Picture your toes from the inside, filled with muscles, tendons, and bones, all working in concert. Feel a sense of gratitude and thankfulness to them. As you breathe, you may even visualize them filling up with the breath, bringing even more awareness to this part of the body. Do this now for a few moments. When you are ready to move on to the next part of the foot, exhale to release your attention on the toes.

   Optionally, if you want, you may take a moment to send gratitude and appreciation to each part of the body as you go through this exercise.

3) **Take time to now breathe into the soles of your feet, to the balls of the feet and the heel.** Bring full awareness to this part of the feet. Feel any sensations in the soles. Sense the tendons and tissue that are below

the skin. Notice any feelings or signals from inside this part of the body. Again, you can optionally give thanks to the soles of your feet for supporting your body and for allowing you to feel sensations as you walk and move and stay active. Or, you can just continue to sense each part of the body. Again, exhale to release awareness on this part of the body.

4) **Now, with your next breath, you will carry awareness down to the ankles, taking time to fully experience any sensations that are present.** You can imagine the inside of this part of your body, how it is both flexible and strong enough to help you pivot and change directions. Allow yourself to let go of any sensation so as to contact the next sensation as it appears. In this way you can contact new sensations as they appear in this moment, and the next, and the next. If your mind wanders off at any time, that's okay. Just notice where your mind has gone—you can label it as "mind wandering" or "thinking," and then bring your attention back to the moment-by-moment focus of the ankles. You can label wherever the mind goes—if it has a picture in the mind's eye, just label that as "seeing." If a sound hijacks your mind, just label that as "hearing," then return to the sensing of the body.

5) **Continue to move up the left side of the body.** Take a breath and picture that breath bringing awareness to each part as you sense the shin/calf, knee, hand, lower arm, upper arm, shoulders, back, spine, neck, and then the head (face, skull, and scalp). After reaching the top of the body, you can complete the body scan by moving down the right side of the body until you reach the toes of the right foot.

6) **The extremities can be surfed or, optionally, you can also scan internal body parts, including the heart, intestines, stomach, genitals, kidneys, liver, spine, and brain, as well as other sense organs that assist in your well-being.**

Feel your connection to each of these parts that help to make a joyful and fulfilling life possible.

7) **When you have completed this practice by addressing all your body, let yourself rest for a few moments in the presence of it.** Give thanks and ask for your body to guide you in doing what is best for it. Let your body know that you will pay attention to the signals it sends you, and that you will follow up any warning signals by getting check-ups and taking care of it through learning about health and preventive measures. By now, you may really be smiling and ready to face the day (or night, as the case may be). This is a wonderful ancient practice that will help you find the strength to do what is right for your body—and the rest of you.

In Conclusion:

During the day, be more aware of your body; it really will let you know when it is happy and when it is not. I know several people, for example, who have told me that they feel less energetic when they drink too much caffeine. It is easy to make corrections if you take the time to become good friends with your body.

Reflections: How can you make the body scan part of a daily practice? When do you think would be a good time to use this?

_____

_____

_____

_____

_____

_____

What will be the biggest challenge you face in implementing the body scan?

_____

_____

_____

_____

_____

Surfing the Body practice is a powerful grounding method. But it needn't be used in the full form described above. How might you adapt this to create the instant, American-style one-minute body scan for greeting the body in the morning or anytime during the day?

_____

_____

_____

_____

_____

Tool #42
Attitude of Acceptance

THOUGHTS FOR THERAPISTS

At times, the energy and emotion with which we resist a situation or condition in our lives may create as much suffering as the very condition itself. Unwillingness, unawareness, or denial of facing one's condition or situation does not help. It only leaves us destined to repeat old behaviors or maladaptive patterns over and over. With acceptance, we gain the willingness to accept our condition and the freedom to move forward in a new, often healthier, way.

Acceptance, though, is sometimes misunderstood as meaning resignation. In truth, they are very different concepts. Resignation is a way of giving up and feeling hopeless in the face of pain, a limitation, or an abuse. It is an unwillingness to move forward or make changes. Acceptance, by contrast, is a choice. With acceptance, one is aware of a difficult situation while bringing an understanding of what one can control and what one can't.

We may have acceptance of the difficult emotions that come from pain and physical limitations—the anger, frustration, and feelings of helplessness. But we may also find acceptance for ways to live in pain that can still invite joy and meaning. Acceptance is a powerful means of finding meaning during any kind of loss. The handout here is designed to help move one more towards acceptance.

TIPS FOR WORKING WITH CLIENTS

- Help clients understand the difference between acceptance and resignation.
  - Acceptance may not change a situation, but it can change how one feels about it and responds to it.
- Three other related practices that go a long way toward supporting the wisdom of acceptance are the following:
  - Tool #43, *Bear Meditation*
  - Tool #48, *Loving-Kindness Affirmation*
  - Tool #50, *At Peace with Pain*

HANDOUT: ATTITUDE OF ACCEPTANCE

Have you ever fought against something in your life that you couldn't change? Maybe when you were 15 years old you wanted to drive a car, but the driving age was older than that. Or, maybe you didn't get accepted to the college you wanted. Or perhaps you lost out on the job you interviewed for. Yes, you could stay mad, upset, and frustrated, or you could accept it and move on. Acceptance is the ability to move forward, and it means that you can still find another job, go to another college, or wait to get older so you can finally drive.

Acceptance is what is in our control. It can even be the attitude with which we deal with unwanted situations that we cannot control or change. A loss of physical health and pain are two such unwanted conditions. By answering the questions below, you will see if an attitude of acceptance might have a place in helping you. Keep in mind that acceptance is a choice, and is very different from resignation. Don't confuse the two. Resignation means giving up and being unwilling or unable to see what you can and can't control.

The Serenity Prayer, a cornerstone of 12-Step programs, eloquently makes this point:

> *God grant me the serenity*
> *To accept the things I cannot change;*
> *Courage to change the things I can;*
> *And the wisdom to know the difference.*

Instructions:

How you choose to use language around your situation and pain can influence how you feel. Answer the following questions to explore the concept of acceptance, as well as to find new ways to work with language. Acceptance is not an answer, but a place from which change can begin.

When you think about your pain or physical limitations, how do you describe to others how it is affecting your life? What key words really tell the story?

_____

_____

_____

_____

_____

_____

How does this description make you feel? What emotions result from your telling others of your pain?

_____

_____

_____

_____

_____

_____

_____

If you could give a name to your pain or health condition, what would that be? You could name it after a movie character, a color, an object, or even a feeling. Choose any name you want, and feel free to get creative.

_____

_____

_____

_____

How does this chosen name make you feel? Victimized? Hopeless? Hopeful? Empowered? Sad? Demoralized? Intimidated? Powerful? In control? Out of control?

_____

_____

_____

_____

If the previous name you came up with for your pain or health condition produced negative feelings, come up with a new name. Think of a word or name that might make you laugh or feel less negative. Again, draw upon TV, film and other ideas, as well as objects. See if it's possible to find a name that makes you smile.

_____

_____

_____

_____

What would it be like not to fight or go to war with your pain or condition?

_____

_____

_____

What part or parts of your pain or condition could you start to accept? For example, could you listen your pain like you listen to a dear family member? Could you care for your pain like you might care for an injured friend? Could you look upon your pain like you gaze at the photo of a heroic person you admire?

_____

_____

_____

_____

_____

How might an attitude of acceptance change how you feel? How would it change the story you would use to describe your pain or condition? Write that new story below—even if you're not entirely committed to it or believe it. Just see what it would look and sound like.

_____

_____

_____

_____

_____

What advice would your wise, nurturing self give you about learning to accept?

_____

_____

_____

_____

_____

Tool #43
Bear Meditation

THOUGHTS FOR THERAPISTS

When we can't find a rational answer for our problems, meditation offers another pathway. While meditating isn't a panacea that will make pain disappear, it does offer other benefits. For some, it can bring about a sense of peace, equanimity, and resolution. It can deepen one's understanding through a flash of insight. And, it can help one to be present and bear witness to one's pain in a caring and compassionate way.

This meditation can be done in session, and may best work for persons who have a spiritual or religious background or inclination.

TIPS FOR WORKING WITH CLIENTS

- Use the instructions as a readable script to guide the client through the *Bear Meditation*.
  - Pause at the appropriate places to give the client time to experience the meditation.
- This practice is helpful for clients whether or not they identify a belief in God or a higher power. They can imagine their own wise and nurturing self as the source for what they tap into.
  - Meditative practices have been used in all traditions. Here are two other meditations that can provide some much needed comfort:
    - Tool #48, *Loving-Kindness Affirmation*
    - Tool #50, *At Peace with Pain*
- Let clients know that the purpose of this meditation is not to extinguish pain but to help them accept, understand, and work with it in a new light.

HANDOUT: BEAR MEDITATION

In the film *The Big Lebowski*, there is a scene where the Stranger says to the Jeff Bridges' character the Dude, the following words: "Sometimes you eat the bear, and sometimes, well, he eats you."

The bear can be any difficult, unresolved situation in your life—like the pain you must endure. The interesting thing about bears is this: Your attitude toward the bear can make all the difference in the world! If you provoke the bear and try to get it to leave, it may attack you and try to make a meal of you. You might try to have patience for the bear, try to outlast it and maybe it will move on. You could even try to befriend the bear, so you can the bear can co-exist. Another approach might be to just be present with compassion for both you and the bear—to "bear witness" so to speak.

So, which approach would you choose?

Instructions:

Follow the steps below to help you get help for dealing with the bear. Use this *Bear Meditation* not so much to find a solution, but more to acknowledge your willingness to be open to hearing a new perspective in dealing with it.

1) Find a quiet place where you can sit in silence as long as you need. Before starting, set the following intention: "May my higher power listen with love and compassion. May my higher power not judge me. May it point me toward a wise path filled with deeper awareness, meaning, and self-compassion."

2) Have a heart-to-heart with the higher power in your life about your pain. Spend a few moments to think about this higher power. A higher power can be anything from a belief in God to the wise, nurturing self within, or anything in between—even a wise and kind being like Mother Teresa, St. Francis, the Buddha, or any other admired individual. If you want, you can visualize your higher power seated opposite you.

   State how the *bear* is affecting your life. Let your higher power know about your fears, worries, emotions, and concerns. As you tell your story, know that your higher power is listening intently. In addition, know that your higher power instantly came to be by your side to you right now because he or she cares deeply about your well-being.

3) Let your higher power know that this difficulty is something that you can't easily handle on your own, and that you have come to ask for help. Visualize your higher power as fully understanding and appreciating the wisdom you have in seeking assistance. Take a few moments to feel how nice it is not to carry the heavy weight and burden of dealing with the *bear* all by yourself. Feel the lightness of this.

4) Ask the higher power for courage to just 'sit' with the *bear*. Do this without expectations just so you might understand the bear better. The higher power may help you here, to just give you another viewpoint, a wise way of being with this. Surrender to whatever happens. If there is sadness, give that to the higher power to hold. Whatever happens, know that the higher power is there with you, supporting you, and sending you love and compassion each moment. Sit for as long as you need.

5) You are not yet done. For now, you will do something you may have thought to be impossible. You will switch seats and positions with your higher power. This doesn't mean that you *are* this higher power, but that you can view yourself with care, and compassion, and love through the eyes of the higher power. From that vantage point, see what it's like to look at you. See your courage, appreciate your strength, witness your wisdom. You only need to do this for a few seconds. Now, return your presence to your body.

6) Lastly, say a blessing of gratitude and thanks for how your higher self made itself available to you—and how it will continue to do so anytime that you need assistance in the future or whenever you want to do another meditation.

Reflections: How did the *Bear Meditation* change your approach to the bear? What did you learn about it or yourself?

_____

_____

_____

_____

_____

_____

_____

What is it like to know that you can tap into your higher power when needed? How do you think this can be of use?

_____

_____

_____

_____

_____

_____

_____

Tool #44
Focusing Away

THOUGHTS FOR THERAPISTS

The most human part of the brain, the prefrontal cortex, has many amazing capabilities. One natural talent possessed by the prefrontal cortex is the ability to have selective focus. That means we can broaden attention or narrow attention. This ability is what helps pilots land planes during sudden emergencies. The pilots are totally focused on what they are doing—they aren't thinking about picking up groceries later that day or checking their email! They've been expertly trained to follow a back-up plan, and they go about it methodically.

Fortunately, we can have a back-up plan when pain gets too intense. There are many stories of people who have had minor surgical operations or gone to the dentist without getting anesthesia. They accomplish this because they are able to distance from the pain by focusing their attention elsewhere. In the same way, *Focusing Away* is effective at turning attention toward something pleasant. Best of all, it can be practiced by anyone because it utilizes all the different learning styles.

TIPS FOR WORKING WITH CLIENTS

- Along with *Focusing Away,* consider incorporating the following practices as ways to refocus attention toward the positive and to cope with pain:
  - Tool #25, *My Favorite Things*
  - Tool #31, *The Lightness of Laughter*
- Even if someone is unable to actively practice a hobby, problem-solve with the client to find an activity that is related to that pleasant activity.

HANDOUT: FOCUSING AWAY

Did you ever hear the blare of a siren while driving in a car? Did you notice that your focus narrows on the sound. Where is the siren? Is it a fire truck, ambulance, or police car? Which direction is it coming from? And, in that moment, you were probably oblivious to many of the other sights and sounds around you. That's because of the power of focusing.

In the same way, magicians use your own ability to focus against you—by distracting you and getting you to focus on what they want. This is called misdirection, and it is done so you don't notice where they are *really* placing that object that they just made disappear. For this *Focusing Away* practice, you will get to be your own magician. In this magic trick you will see if you can make your pain disappear—or at least lessen—by focusing strongly on other items in your environment, as well as actions that draw your attention elsewhere.

Instructions:

To help augment your *Focusing Away* abilities, you are going to create a *Comfort Box*. This box that will contain all the different ideas and ways that you can find comfort in order to create some distance from pain and help you pay attention to those things that can bring some kind of pleasure.

Anything can be in a Comfort Box. It can include actual items, such as a meditation or music CD that you find uplifting, a lavender scented candle, or even a chocolate nugget. It can also contain notes that tell you what to do, such as looking at a photo album that makes you smile. Look at the categories below, and circle those items that you feel will positively grab your attention. If something has worked in the past, include it in your comfort box.

What does a Comfort Box look like? Anything you want it to be! It can be a cardboard box that you have decorated or labeled. It can be a jewelry box or any container used for another purpose. You can decorate it, color it, and make it expressive.

COMFORT ACTIVITIES:

(Circle the activities that you know will focus you away—even to a small extent. When done, write your selections on a sheet of paper to put in the Comfort Box. Tailor the activity to whatever is manageable for you. A walk in Nature, for example, might mean walking 20 feet out the front door and noticing the grass, hedges, plants, and flowers before walking back).

Take a walk in Nature	Meet a friend	Eat a meal
Sit in Nature	Prepare a nice meal	Eat an enjoyable food
Appropriate exercise	Call a friend	Email or text a friend
Read a favorite book	Watch a favorite film	Listen to an uplifting song
Draw or sketch	Look at a flower	Smell a rose
Do a crossword puzzle	Do a Sudoku puzzle	Read the funnies
Read a poem	Read scripture	Write (anything that is fun)
Stretch	Breathe deeply	Smile (just for no reason)
Watch a favorite TV show	Pet an animal	Play solitaire
Play cards with someone	Pray/meditate	Play a game (like Scrabble)
Blow bubbles	Learn one new thing	Write a positive memory

Practice your vocabulary   Drink a cool drink   Drink a warm drink

Put on favorite clothes   Think of favorite person   Find your favorite color/art

Enjoy your favorite room   Sit in a comfy chair   Laugh with favorite show

Reflections: In the space below, add other comfort activities that will help you focus away.

_____

_____

_____

<u>COMFORT ITEMS:</u>   Circle the Comfort Items that appeal to you.

Scented candle	Favorite film DVD	Favorite upbeat music CD
Small favorite food treat	Favorite book	Favorite poem
Favorite inspiring quote	Aromatherapy	Photos (friends, family)
Bubble bath	Bubble-blower	Favorite hand cream
Favorite keepsake	Favorite jewelry	Precious letter
Journal of good memories	Puzzle book	Prayer beads
Spiritual object or icon	Favorite scripture	Favorite childhood toy
Playing cards	Favorite beverage (hot chocolate, lemonade)	

Reflections: In the space below, add other comfort items that will help you focus away.

_____

_____

_____

To see how good a magician you are and how well this works for you, you will rate your level of pain before and after using a comfort activity or item. This way, you can find out what works best. Use a 1-10 scale where 1 is the lowest pain and 10 is the highest. You may find that certain activities/items work best when pain is initially lower, while others work best when pain is initially higher. Use the table here as a guide, or make your own. Remember to use the activity or item for a long enough time to make it effective.

Pain Before (1-10)	Comfort Activity/Item	Pain After (1-10)

Tool #45
Decentralizing Pain

THOUGHTS FOR THERAPISTS

If there's one thing that makes pain difficult to work with, it is how it is so very personally felt and experienced. Pain belongs to the sufferer. They own it, as much as anything else they possess. It may be unwanted, but it is still experienced as belonging to the *I*, the *me*, the *my*, and the *mine*. This personal experience fuses the pain sufferer with the pain and, often, it can be hard to separate the two: *My pain is indistinguishable from me, and I am my pain.* Once fused, there is constant negative reactivity to the pain trigger, which can occur instantly. What is more, there is the emotional suffering that comes from "buying" this pain as one's identity.

Creating space from the pain by not viewing it so personally can take out the blame, the shame, the anger, and other negative emotions associated with pain. Of course, this is easier said than done. Our proclivity to process our stories from the I-centric point of view is strongly conditioned. That's not to say, however, that we can't learn a new way of experiencing and broadening out the story toward a more decentralized perspective.

One mindfulness method for working with craving, emotions, and triggers of any kind is the practice of looking and observing at an experience from the third person point of view. This takes practice, but it can be a real eye-opener for those who engage in it. With a therapist's wise guidance, you can help someone through the process of decentralizing pain. The *Decentralizing Pain* handout here is helpful when first explained and used in session.

TIPS FOR WORKING WITH CLIENTS

- Consider starting with Tool #42, *Attitude of Acceptance* as a way to broaden the story of pain, which will open the door for the *Decentralizing Pain* practice. These two mindful awareness practices will work well together.
- Read through the handout and try it yourself before trying it with the client. It will be a lot easier to grasp and explain to someone else if you first experience telling your

story in the ways that are described below. (You will also be able to empathize with how difficult it can be to tell a story in a decentralized way, without using the words *I*, *me*, *my*, and *mine*).

- It is important to go through the *Decentralizing Pain* handout in session before having the patient try it alone because the therapist's role as the "engaged listener" is critical to the decentralizing process.
  - Go through the entire handout at one sitting, from parts one through four.
- Be sure to process the feelings that come from doing the decentralizing practice. There is often a sense of relief that comes from not being so tightly wound up with the I-centric story.

HANDOUT: DECENTRALIZING PAIN

This handout is designed to get you thinking about pain and the experience of pain in a different way. But first, to illustrate a point, answer the following question as a full sentence. The question is this: *What food did you eat this morning and how did you like it?*

That was easy, wasn't it? Now, did you use the words "I," "me," "my," or "mine" in answering that question? Of course you did! That's normal, because we typically take a very personal, or "I-centric" view of things. This is how we talk about and share our world and experiences.

But what happens when we talk about *my pain*? What happens when we buy into the pain as being our own? Now, this is not to imply that you are *not* the one experiencing it. Of course you are. However, what this practice suggests is that it is possible to view and experience pain—or anything for that matter—from a more neutral and less judgmental perspective. In other words, it would be like an impartial witness who was noticing what was occurring and just describing it without any personal stake in what is happening. Have you ever wondered how taking an "impartial witness" perspective that might change your feelings about the pain?

Instructions:

This practice will let you experience the story of your pain from that impartial witness viewpoint. There are four parts to this exercise, which begins with a *Warm-up Story*.

1) *Warm-up Story—Personal Point of View:* For the next three minutes you will describe a recent memorable meal that you had. It's best if this meal was shared with others and had some kind of an emotional component— either very positive or negative. Now, describe that story in detail—what you ate, how the food tasted and whether you liked or didn't like it, who you were with, whether you enjoyed or didn't enjoy the conversation, what you talked about, and the place where you had the meal. Did you eat more than you wanted? How did that feel for you? (Alternatively, write down the story here if there is no one to tell it to).

_____

_____

_____

_____

_____

_____

_____

2) *Warm-up Story—Decentralized Point of View:* Excellent. You just shared a story very much from the personal "I" point of view. Now, you will share the *identical* story in a very different way. This time, you will tell the story, but *without* using the words by "I," "me," "my," or "mine" in the telling. That's right—you're going to try to decentralize your story! This is not an easy thing to do, so here are a few suggestions. When telling the story in this way, don't use a pronoun such as "he" or "she" or "this person" to represent you. That would be like using "I". Instead, talk about the experiences, such as "There was the experience of *the body* walking and

sitting down at the table," or "*the mouth* tasted the hamburger and noticed how juicy it was," or "*the eyes* saw the white tablecloth," or "*the stomach* felt uncomfortably tight after eating," or "there was a conversation that was very interesting," etc.

Do you see how it is possible to tell the same story from a third person perspective?

It's important when you first practice this to tell your story to an engaged listener. The listener has a very important and specific job. The listener will not interrupt while listening with interest. Most importantly, the listener will be paying attention for the words "I," "me," "my," or "mine" that you may use without even knowing it. Upon hearing any of these words, the listener will simply raise their hand to let you know that you used the word. Then you can rephrase your story.

Again, this is not easy, and you *don't have to be perfect in not using those words*. The point of telling your story this way is to help you learn that your experience of having a meal (or of pain) can be viewed in this decentralized way. You are always able to go back to your very personal, "I-centric" viewpoint after this practice.

At this time you will share your same meal story without using the words "I," "me," "my," or "mine" for the next three minutes, and the engaged listener will keep time for you. Are you ready? Start now. (Alternatively, if you can't find someone to tell the decentralized story with, write that version of the story below).

_____

_____

_____

_____

_____

_____

_____

_____

Reflections: How challenging was it for you to tell your story without using the personal "I," "me," "my," or "mine" words?

_____

_____

_____

What did it feel like to experience your story from this more neutral point of view? Was it more descriptive? Did it have less negative emotional feeling for you?

_____

_____

_____

_____

What is one helpful or positive thing you noticed by shifting into the impartial spectator point of view?

_____

_____

_____

_____

3) *Story of Pain—Personal Point of View:* For three minutes you will tell the very *personal* story of an experience where you felt pain. This could be the story of your morning, such as waking up. Or, it could be the story of how pain limited your ability to do something you wanted to do (see a friend, take part in some activity, etc). . Use as many "I," "me," "my," or "mine" words as you like! (If you don't have someone to share this story with, write down your experience below).

_____

_____

_____

_____

_____

_____

_____

_____

4) *Story of Pain—Decentralized Point of View:* You've already had practice telling a story without the words "I," "me," "my," or "mine." For the next three minutes you will share the identical pain story that you just described, but from the very neutral, non-judging and impartial perspective of an interested witness. Again, the engaged listener will keep time and raise their hand to let you know if you've used the words "I," "me," "my," or "mine" during your story. If so, just rephrase and start again, describing the experiences in parts of the body. Even the word "pain" is a judgment of sorts, so you might consider using the word "sensation," then describing that sensation as well as you can—such as "tightness" "vise-like" "tension" "wave-like" or whatever words describe the sensation that you felt in that moment. Remember to describe your surroundings and other experiences in detail.

By the way, you can still mention negative thoughts that were part of the pain story. From the observer perspective you might describe that as, "The mind kept repeating the negative thought that . . ." or "there was the feeling of frustration and tightness in the gut," or "the mind said the words "I wish things were different." In this way, you can know what is in the mind, and what is in the body.

(If you don't have an engaged listener, journal your decentralized story of pain in the space below).

_____

_____

_____

_____

_____

_____

_____

_____

Reflections: After having had some practice, what was it like to again tell a story from the decentralized perspective?

_____

_____

_____

_____

What did it feel like to experience your story of pain from this more neutral point of view? Were you able to notice how thoughts or commentary from the mind had a role in your pain story? It can be helpful to know that just because you "have" a thought doesn't mean you have to "buy" it or decide to purchase it as your own.

_____

_____

_____

_____

What is one helpful or positive thing you noticed by shifting into the impartial spectator point of view for your story of pain?

_____

_____

_____

_____

How do you think this shift could be useful? When could you practice telling the story in this decentralized way— even if as a reminder that you have a choice about how to experience your story of pain?

_____

_____

_____

_____

Tool #46
Reaching Beyond the Cocoon of Pain

> ## LEARNING STYLES
>
> The following learning styles are compatible with this practice:
>
> Verbal-Linguistic
>
> Social-Interpersonal

THOUGHTS FOR THERAPISTS

Pain can cause a protective cocoon to form around someone. Such a cocoon may have a survival purpose because it may help to conserve emotional and physical energy during a time of crisis. Understandably, pain can make one pull back inside his or her own shell and retreat from the outside world, especially from relationships. Pain can dramatically shift roles in relationships, change how intimacy or even touch are experienced, and produce a deep river of guilt or resentment.

How does one go about restoring or repairing relationships after a long stay in the cocoon? Recovery from pain is very much about reaching out of the cocoon to start a new life. Just as the butterfly's exodus from the cocoon is a long and often difficult progression, restoring relationships can also be a tenuous and delicate process.

The *Reaching Beyond the Cocoon of Pain* is an inventory and exploration for those persons who may still be in pain, or who are recovering from it, and who want to take stock of how it has affected the relationships in their lives. If someone has been in their cocoon for any length of time, it can be scary to leave it behind. Trust and openness are essential qualities to breaking through a cocoon of pain that has hardened with fear, anger, and other powerful emotions.

TIPS FOR WORKING WITH CLIENTS

- Combine *Reaching Beyond the Cocoon of Pain* with another highly supportive and encouraging practice for making connections:
  - Tool #26, *Savoring Success—Past, Present, and Future*
- Investigate the client's history and their methods for connecting with partners in the past for clues as to how to successfully reach beyond the cocoon of pain.
  - Use this handout not just for those who have withdrawn because of a cocoon of physical pain, but for emotional cocoons, such as those caused by divorce, depression, and grief, etc.

- The client's readiness and motivation to reconnect with significant others after an illness is an important element to consider as you engage the client in the *Reaching Beyond the Cocoon of Pain* exploration and handout.

- After dealing with the client's fears and concerns about restoring a relationship, it may be helpful to establish realistic goals and timelines for making this happen.

- There are many pathways for reaching out of the cocoon of pain. This includes:
  - Work relationships
  - Family relationships
  - Friendships

HANDOUT: REACHING BEYOND THE COCOON OF PAIN

Any kind of sustained experience pain—physical or emotional—can cause us to isolate and withdraw over time. Pain can be like a cocoon that separates us from others. Stuck in the cocoon, we marshal all our energy to deal with and mange the pain. Meanwhile, we may have little or few resources available for others. Through no fault of our own we isolate, and sometimes the cocoon is thick enough to keep others out.

The handout here is intended as an exploration of how your cocoon of pain has affected your relationships and offers some suggestions for what you can do to start *Reaching Beyond the Cocoon of Pain* to restore and re-establish connections with others.

Instructions: Reflect on the questions/reflections that follow. Remember that there are no wrong answers here. If you have been hidden in the cocoon for any length of time, it can be scary to reach out.

Completing this handout is an act of courage on your part. It requires openness, faith, and trust to peek out of that cocoon, to tear open the walls that have held you in a difficult time. But no cocoon is meant to be permanent. Every butterfly must break out of its temporary home in order to fly free.

Reflections: How long have you been in your cocoon of pain? What purpose did the cocoon serve for you? Did it serve a useful purpose of any kind?

_____

_____

_____

_____

_____

How did the cocoon transform or change over time? Did it grow thicker? Was it darker inside? Was it more resistant to things outside it?

_____

_____

_____

_____

_____

How did being in the cocoon affect your relationships over time—home, work, friends, etc.?

_____

_____

_____

_____

_____

What is your single greatest worry, fear, or concern about leaving the cocoon?

_____

_____

_____

_____

What relationships would you like to re-establish after your time in the cocoon?

_____

_____

_____

_____

What roles, if any, have shifted as a result of your being in the cocoon? (For example, a spouse might have had to take on more daily responsibilities as a result of her/his partner being in the cocoon).

_____

_____

_____

_____

What is one, small, simple way you could reach out from the cocoon to a person you care about? Any idea is useful, and the more you can come up with, the better. (This could include anything like, a call, a kind touch on the shoulder, a smile, any act of caring, making a meal for that person, etc).

_____

_____

_____

_____

How can you use the small, caring actions and strategies mentioned above in a consistent way? It takes time to rebuild when you reach out of the cocoon! Have patience and persistence. How can you journal or keep track of your efforts at reaching out of the cocoon? Notice the results, too, and how it makes you feel to fly more freely.

_____

_____

_____

_____

Tool #47
Lessons from Nature

THOUGHTS FOR THERAPISTS

In her thoughtful and wise book, *How to Train a Wild Elephant*, Jan Chozen-Bays, M.D., writes, "Mindfulness of our continuous, inter-breathing relationship with trees and green plants can provide us with a vivid awareness of our interconnectedness with all beings . . . If a living being doesn't catch our notice by being noisy, moving about, looking soulfully into our eyes, or being dangerous, we stop noticing it." If you have stopped noticing Nature, then you may be missing out on one of the greatest shows known to man—and it's available daily without buying an expensive ticket or requiring 3-D film glasses.

Nature teaches by virtue of just being what it is—authentic and real. There's nothing phony about it. It knows what it needs to do, and it doesn't need to question its motives. Chozen-Bays also makes the point that a single, young tree, for example, delivers as much cooling as do ten average room-sized air conditioning units from the big box store down the street. Trees also create micro-environments, by cooling in the summer and keeping things warmer in the winter.

As humans possessing eyes, noses, ears, hands, and feet, we tend to relate to beings that are most like ourselves. For example, we don't think of insects in very warm, endearing terms, do we? We tend to be primate and mammal-centric. But if we were to raise our arms up to the sky, letting our fingers stretch out like branches, we might discover that we kind of resemble a tree. How beautiful is it to think that humans are actually moveable trees—with feet. Now, with that in mind, let's see what lessons our tree-cousins can share with us.

TIPS FOR WORKING WITH CLIENTS

- For those clients who are contemplative and connect with this *Lessons from Nature* practice, introduce them to the following similarly oriented handouts:
  - Tool #15, *Sky Gazing with Nature*
  - Tool #34, *Turning Down the Volume with Nature*

HANDOUT: LESSONS FROM NATURE

The Benefits of Paying Attention to Nature

Have you ever found yourself immersed in the wonder and splendor of Nature? There are trees, for example, that are known to be several thousands of years old. Trees are not only the largest living organisms on Earth, but we depend on them for our very survival. More importantly, they have a lot to teach us—if only we paid more attention to them.

Instructions: Read the story below and then take an inventory of how Nature might help you find lessons about dealing with the pain in your life.

What follows is true story of one man—let's call him Jerry—who got a surprising lesson just because he decided to go outside and watch the trees one day.

> *Jerry worked at an office that had become a depressing and sad place to go to each day. There had been many lay-offs, and Jerry had seen several of his friends and associates let go. Soon, Jerry figured, his time was coming.*
>
> *Meanwhile, Jerry worried and fretted endlessly about this, until the concern permeated into all areas of his life. Jerry stopped talking to people at work and closed the door to his office. He felt like a prisoner waiting for an execution, and he let it affect his life negatively, to the point where he became severely depressed.*
>
> *One morning, to take a break from the oppressive feeling of the office, Jerry stepped outside to a small courtyard that was enclosed by the building. It wasn't anything spectacular, just a few nondescript trees and some small bushes. Jerry sat on a wooden bench, and before long his attention was grabbed by Nature around him. He forgot about all his troubles at work. For a moment he wasn't thinking about what the day he would be called into his boss's office or how he would find another job after being let go. He wasn't regretting how his retirement plans would be dashed. He wasn't frowning about what a disappointment he would be to his family and his wife. Instead, he was one-hundred percent engaged in the drama and story of Nature that unfolded before him.*
>
> *It came to him like a sudden bolt of lightning. There it was, right before him. The answer he was seeking.*
>
> *Jerry's eyes were peeled on the thick, brownish vines of ivy that were clinging to the tree trunks. He could see where the gardeners had cut these off. But the ivy started growing again up the side of the tree. It didn't just give up and stop living because the gardener came along with a pair of shears. The ivy had no fear of failure, and no worry, because it was just doing what it was supposed to do, and it always found a way to keep moving forward.*
>
> *Suddenly, Jerry had a powerful realization:* Even if my job comes to an end tomorrow, I'll find a way to keep growing and living, just like that vine.

Reflections: Have you ever had an "aha" experience with Nature—just like Jerry did in the story above? What was it like to read a story where hopelessness was transformed into hope?

_____

_____

_____

_____

_____

_____

From your experience of Nature, trees, and plants, is there any observation you have made that is applicable to your story of pain? Is there a lesson from Nature that can give you a sense of hope or find a different way to experience pain?

_____

_____

_____

_____

_____

_____

_____

How can you sit with Nature as a practice—whether daily, every other day, or once a week?

_____

_____

_____

_____

_____

_____

_____

Paradoxically, the secret to tapping into Nature's wisdom may be in just letting it be and not expecting an answer. Still, it can be valuable to set an intention to be present and open to the lessons that Nature may invite. In the space below, write down your intention—it only has to be a sentence or two—that clearly states your wish to open to whatever lessons Nature is willing to offer. You can imagine this lesson as coming from whatever source you want—from a higher power, God, your own wise self, Mother Earth, and so on.

_____

_____

_____

_____

_____

_____

Tool #48
Loving-Kindness Affirmation

THOUGHTS FOR THERAPISTS

Suffering is one thing that all humans have in common. (Hopefully, so is *joy*) Still, as a human being it is not possible to avoid loss of some kind. Possessing a human body means being subject to illness, frailty, aging, and ultimately, death. Of course, trying to deny, resist, or pretend that this doesn't exist is just another form of suffering. There seems to be no way out of this mess, and yet, there is a way to bring meaning to loss and pain. It is called compassion—whose original meaning translates as "to be with suffering."

To know suffering means that we can try to relieve suffering. Unlike empathy, through which we can step into the emotional shoes of another person, compassion impels us toward being available to reduce the suffering of others through selfless action. Indeed, over twenty-five percent, or one-quarter of all Americans, volunteer or give service to those in need. While some researchers believe compassion is an instinct that leads to survival, others believe that it can be taught. Either way, more compassion—and self-compassion—is greatly needed.

Researcher Richard Davidson—director of The Center for Investigating Healthy Minds and author of *The Emotional Life of Your Brain* (co-authored with Sharon Begley)—has put the Dalai Lama's monks into magnetic resonance imaging machines to see if brain function was altered in those who have practiced ten- thousand hours or longer of compassion meditation. His work shows that intensive training in compassion produces significant changes in brain function. Davidson has also found that compassion can be learned, and that it results in altruistic behavior in subjects who undertake compassion training.

What do we do with this knowledge? We can put it to use by using the ancient loving-kindness meditation or affirmation practice. This practice generates compassion toward oneself and others, as well as forgiveness—both attributes that can firmly assist those struggling with pain and the loss of physical well-being.

TIPS FOR WORKING WITH CLIENTS

- *The Loving-Kindness Affirmation* is closely related to Tool #50, *At Peace with Pain*, which is another meditation that can be used to engender warm feelings of love and understanding. Share both of these with clients as a nice boxed set.

- Before working with loving-kindness, it is important to understand the religious or spiritual background of your client.
    - While loving-kindness was originally an ancient Buddhist practice, the words are considered by attachment researchers to be "security priming words"—that is, words that prime the limbic emotional core of the brain for feelings of safety, trust, and openness.
    - When exposed to certain words, such as *love, closeness, safety*, etc., people have experienced more openness and trust toward others. To be described in a more secular way, this meditation can be described as a security priming.
    - This meditation is about the deep wish for one's well-being, and that can be imagined as coming from any source—as a blessing, as an affirmation, as coming from any higher power or from God, etc.

- Work with clients in adapting the words in this meditation in appropriate ways. For example:
    - The words "May I be . . ." could be transformed into an active choice by stating, "I choose to be . . ."
    - The meditation could be stated as an affirmation by stating, "I will be . . ." or "I am . . ."
    - Other words can be added to the actual meditation, such as "May I be *loved, accepted, understood, forgiven, pain-free*," etc.

- What follows in the handout can be used as a script for guiding the client through this practice for the first time.

- Practicing this meditation can be a powerful and emotional experience. Always allow time for processing after using this in a session.
    - Always have the client state loving-kindness for themselves first, *then* afterwards send it out to others.

HANDOUT: LOVING-KINDNESS AFFIRMATION

In his book *Works of Love,* Danish philosopher and theologian Søren Kierkegaard shared some wisdom on the essence of love. He wrote:

> *To cheat oneself out of love is the most terrible deception;*
> *it is an eternal loss for which there is no reparation,*
> *either in time or in eternity.*

As someone grappling with pain—either physical or emotional (maybe both)—it may be hard to think about the idea of love. But the affirmation practiced in these pages is not like the love you may be thinking of. It is not the flavor of love that is romantic, sentimental, or nostalgic—dependent on one person or a specific memory. Rather, this is the deeply profound and compassionate wish for the well-being of all persons.

It is predicated on the basis that all beings deserve this non-discriminating love, that we all *need* it because all of us have struggled or suffered in some way. Even that person who seems happy and appears to have it all together will deal with loss and pain in life. And so, this practice is a form of compassion—which really means *to be with the suffering of another.*

We begin by developing compassion for ourselves. This is a process, since you may not feel you are deserving of this deep wish for your well-being. If this is the case, you can begin by picturing the young baby, toddler, or child you once were, and who was deserving of this loving meditation. State the words for that part of you.

Offering love and charity toward our neighbors is a central tenant to all wisdom traditions. Key examples of loving-kindness are found in stories of how Jesus, Buddha, and Mohammed all fed the hungry and starving, without discrimination. Whatever your background may be, this is an inclusive practice that anyone can benefit from. In addition, you can see the words here in any way that fits with your religious or spiritual background—as a blessing, a prayer, an affirmation, and so on.

Instructions: Follow along with the words below, stating them to yourself over and over ... *like you really mean it.*

1) BEGIN WITH FORGIVENESS.

We've all been hurt, which is why this practice begins with forgiveness. You may be that parent, for example, who knows you have unintentionally wronged your children and yet hope for the grace of forgiveness. Or, you may have inadvertently hurt someone because you didn't know any better. Whatever the case may be, reflect on the words below. Allow forgiveness to act as a salve for your wounded spirit so that you may let go and move on. By sending forgiveness, you also open the gateway to a more awakened and sensitive behavior—alert to even the subtle consequences of your actions and thoughts. Jesus spoke to this in the Bible (Luke 6:37) when he said, "Do not judge, and you will not be judged. Do not condemn, and you will not be condemned. Forgive, and you will be forgiven."

Repeat the following words once before moving on.

> *May I forgive myself for hurting others.*
> *May others forgive me for hurting them.*
> *May I forgive myself for hurting myself.*

2) SAY LOVING-KINDNESS FOR YOURSELF.

Repeat the following words over and over. Say them until you can feel the words resonating within. This could be for five minutes, for 10, for 30 minutes.

> *May I be safe.*
> *May I be happy.*
> *May I be healthy.*
> *May I be peaceful.*
>
> Optionally, add these words—
> *May I be free from pain, hunger, and suffering.*

3) SAY LOVING-KINDNESS FOR OTHERS.

Next, you will repeat the loving-kindness meditation/affirmation for others. Picture these individuals looking radiant and healthy and happy as you send them this deep wish for their well-being.

Look at the list of six groups below. The top two are self-explanatory, but the "neutral persons" group refers to persons who you may see or interact with from time to time but who you don't really know—such as that person at the checkout stand at the grocery store, that person who lives down the street who you wave to, etc.

The "unfriendly group" represents those persons who are difficult persons in your life. They may have even created pain and abuse. This is a group that presents the greatest challenge for sending out the loving-kindness words. If you find that you can't send to this group, you can stop and start sending love to yourself. Then, where you feel resonance with the words, again start sending loving-kindness to others, starting from the top of the list.

Remember, that even that abuser or difficult person in your life has suffered in some way. Even this person would benefit from such a blessing. In addition, you can know that difficult person does not have to know you are sending these words out to them. In fact, they may not even be alive. Because loving-kindness breaks down the walls of separation between ourselves and others, saying it for others—even those who may have hurt or harmed us—is also beneficial to us! Here are the categories and the way you can repeat the loving-kindness wish of well-being for these groups of persons.

1) Teachers/mentors/guides

2) Family members

3) Friends

4) Neutral persons

5) Unfriendly persons

6) All Persons/living beings/living things without discrimination

Repeat the following loving-kindness words for each of the above groups.

> *May (name here) be safe.*
> *May (name here) be happy.*
> *May (name here) be healthy.*
> *May (name here) be peaceful.*
>
> Optionally, add these words—
> *May (name here) be free from pain, hunger, and suffering.*

4) CONCLUDE WITH A FINAL BLESSING OR WISH FOR OTHERS.

After you have extended loving-kindness to all the six groups, end with following words.

Say the following words once.

> *May suffering ones by suffering-free,*
> *May the fear-struck fearless be,*
> *May grieving ones shed all grief,*
> *May all beings find relief.*

Reflections: What was it like for you to say the loving-kindness meditation or affirmation? Was there any part of this that you found difficult?

_____

_____

_____

_____

The loving-kindness practice takes time and patience. How do you think this could help you move toward forgiveness—either toward yourself or others?

_____

_____

_____

_____

How could you develop an ongoing loving-kindness meditation or affirmation practice? Where would be an ideal place to practice this—where you might be in the solitude of Nature or at a place you design and dedicate to this gentle practice of cultivating peace, kindness, and compassion?

_____

_____

_____

_____

Tool #49
Healing with Music

LEARNING STYLES

The following learning styles are compatible with this practice:

Verbal-Linguistic

Musical-Sound

Bodily-Kinesthetic-Tactile

THOUGHTS FOR THERAPISTS

There is a lot of evidence that the right kind of music can promote healing. One researcher in this field is Dr. Michael Miller, the director of Preventive Cardiology at the University of Maryland Medical Center. In one study, Miller had subjects listen to joyful music that, from previous experience, made the subjects feel positive or gave them a sense of euphoria. These persons were then tested to see if the inner lining of their blood vessels was constricted or relaxed. Relaxation is beneficial because the endothelium, or the inner lining of our blood and lymphatic vessels, is often considered to be the 'gatekeeper' to our circulatory and vascular health.

Miller's research showed that listening to music for 30 minutes caused the blood vessels to expand. (Miller's previous studies used laughter and got similar results). In an interview recorded on National Public Radio, Miller reported that the expansion was "about 25%, which is similar in magnitude to what has previously been observed with aerobic activity."

In terms of brain science, singing a song (or reciting lyrics or reading out loud) engages much of the brain in activity—which may make it harder to focus on things like anxiety and pain. While music can soothe, it may also help the body come in to manage pain and promote healing in some ways that we are just now beginning to understand.

TIPS FOR WORKING WITH CLIENTS

- For those clients who connect with music as one of their key learning styles, consider integrating Tool #29, *Tune Up with Music* with the complementary practice of *Healing with Music*.
- See if a particular song serves as a metaphor, a daily theme, or even as a mantra that the client can use to stay centered.

HANDOUT: HEALING WITH MUSIC

When is the last time you sang a song—just for the fun of it?

A study conducted at Stockholm University in Sweden showed that when amateurs practiced singing, they reduced feelings of stress while experiencing feelings of joy and elation. Interestingly, professional singers didn't get the same benefit, because they were concerned about performance and achievement. Isn't it nice to know you can sing without that pressure? This is singing just for the fun of it.

If you are too shy or unable to sing for any reason whatsoever, don't worry. Simply listening to music has been proven to be beneficial for reducing stress because of its effect on the vascular system. Listening to joyful music actually expands and relaxes your blood vessels and lymphatic vessels.

Try the strategies below and report how they change your experience of pain, stress, or anxiety.

Instructions:

Experiment with each of the musical ideas below to see which words best for you. Sing for at least five minutes at a time. Sing for longer if you feel like it.

Each time you try one of the musical methods below, rate the level of pain or discomfort you feel on a 1-10 scale, with 1 the lowest level and 10 the highest.

After you have finished, make sure to again rate the pain or level of discomfort on a 1-10 scale. This way, you can see which method is most effective at diminishing, managing, or distracting from pain. (Use the Chart below to track your ratings).

1) SING OR HUM A SONG YOU LIKE.

Even if you haven't typically sung songs before, see what it's like to sing one of your favorite songs. You can also hum the song—which gives you the same benefits. Thomas Jefferson was known for humming his favorite Scottish tunes when he was living at Monticello.

Consider singing a song from your past that you enjoyed. If you can't think of the lyrics, look on the Internet where it's pretty easy to locate lyrics of all kinds.

2) SING ALONG WITH MUSIC.

Like going to a karaoke bar, you can enjoy singing along with music. This might help if you don't have the lyrics available.

3) SIMPLY LISTEN TO MUSIC THAT YOU FIND JOYFUL.

Listen to music that makes you feel good. That could mean a feeling of being uplifted or even euphoric. Ideally, listen for 15-minutes or more. If you can move or sway to the sounds, go ahead and let your body move however it wants. Music from artists Randy Newman and Bobby McFerrin seem to bring smiles to faces. Maybe yours?

4) EXPERIMENT WITH DIFFERENT KINDS OF MUSIC.

You may think you only enjoy a particular musical type. But have you listened to any others lately? For example, soothing, classical music has been shown to help persons to heal more quickly after surgery. This could present you with the opportunity to explore and expand your musical tastes. Or, it may confirm your existing choices! Have fun discovering the different forms of music that are available.

PAIN BEFORE	MUSICAL METHOD	PAIN AFTER
In this column, rate the pain level **before** music. Rate mood on a 1-10 scale: 1=low pain; 1=high pain	Singing/Humming; Sing along with Music; Listen to Joyful Music; Types of Music	Rate your pain level again **after** listening to music using the 1-10 scale.

Reflections: What did you discover about music's effectiveness as a way to manage pain? What did you learn about the ability of music to refocus your attention?

_____

_____

_____

_____

Which method of connecting with music worked best to reduce or distract you from pain? Which would you find most portable and useable?

_____

_____

_____

_____

How could you create an ongoing practice for using music to reduce stress and/or pain? What might be the challenges to making this work? What would be one benefit of this practice for you or others in your life?

_____

_____

_____

_____

Tool #50
At Peace with Pain

THOUGHTS FOR THERAPISTS

Being in chronic or severe pain can be an extremely lonely and isolating experience. It's easy for others to say they understand what it's like to be in pain, but that can ring hollow. While pain can't always be avoided or reduced, the feeling of isolation can be lessened through the practice of meditating on benefactors—those persons who care about us. This can provide a sense of strength, and also help those in pain to find support and reach out to others.

This powerful practice is related to the loving-kindness meditation, but it differs in the sense that it invites a feeling of safety and security through visualization. If pain has locked someone in darkness, (as discussed in Tool #46, *Reaching Beyond the Cocoon of Pain*), this meditation offers an important means for letting in the light. This meditation is a coping skill, a powerful means of helping someone come to a greater sense of peace around their condition.

TIPS FOR WORKING WITH CLIENTS

- For clients who find meditation and visualization helpful, the *At Peace with Pain* practice can fit well with two other meditations found in this section for pain. These include:
  - Tool #43, *Bear Meditation*
  - Tool #48, *Loving-Kindness Affirmation*
- Use the instructions in the handout as a guide for leading clients through this practice for the first time.
- Allow time for processing the emotions that come from practicing this in session.

HANDOUT: AT PEACE WITH PAIN

A Comforting Visualization

As much as it may feel that your pain is something others can't understand or fathom, this meditation can help you realize that you are not alone. Being at peace with pain doesn't mean that you are resigned to pain or that you wouldn't want things different with all your heart and mind. But it does mean that you can rest in the peace of mind and comfort that comes from the love and support of others.

The visualization here will let you be surrounded by the love of those who have cared for you and supported you throughout your life—as well as those who you know would offer their loving presence if they could be with you now.

Instructions:

1) **Before starting, set the following intention:** *With this meditation, may I find peace of mind with my pain through the love, support, and comfort of others.*

2) **Find a quiet, safe location where you will not be interrupted for at least 10 minutes.** Close your eyes.

3) **Recall those persons who it feels good to be around.** These are people from your entire life who have held for you the simple wish that you be loved and well. These are folks who have the warmest thoughts and feelings for you, and when you are in their vicinity, you feel safe and good.

   Picture those people, who could be called benefactors, because they care about your present condition, and they wish the best for you. Who are these persons? This could be a family member or a dear friend who made you feel safe and worthwhile. This person could also be one of your grade school teachers, a kindly neighbor, or a camp counselor who you think fondly of. There may have been strangers who have been kind and who possessed a loving presence that you still recall. In addition, add to this group those spiritual persons or mentors who have had your best interests at heart. These could be historical figures, from Jesus and Buddha to Mother Teresa or anyone who you know would have held the deepest wish for your well-being in their heart. These evolved and spiritual beings fully understand your difficult situation, and they would drop everything to be with you at this time—and to lend you support just by being at your side.

   Bring all of these persons to mind. Visualize them smiling and radiant as they surround you—all the while sending you the warm glow of their deepest love and support. They hold the wish for your happiness, safety, joy, health, and peace. They accept and love you completely and unconditionally, just as you are.

   You might experience their unconditional love and unlimited compassion for your difficult situation and wish for your well-being as a soft glow, a warm light that bathes you completely. Like a warm and sweet honeyed syrup, picture it flowing down from the top of the head and spilling to the tips of your toes. Let this unconditional love and concern for you seep down into every cell of your body. Absorb it with each breath you take.

   Allow yourself to open up in order to let in this support, compassion, and love. Should you notice any skeptical or negative thoughts creeping into your mind, just release these—again returning to the deep wish for your well-being.

   If your mind wanders, simply notice that and gently return it to your group of caring and loving supporters, or benefactors. Notice that their love and compassion is not passive at all. It is like a deep, flowing river of energy that moves you and deeply inspires you. How wonderful to be surrounded by so many loving persons . . .

4) **Mentally say the following words for yourself,**

   May I rest in the very compassion, love,
   and support that these individuals hold for me.

May I rest with a sense of abiding peace with my situation,
Knowing that I am always supported by my benefactors.

5) All things are inter-connected. And so, optionally, you can choose to mentally dissolve the separation between yourself your benefactors. Right now, let yourself merge with them as you come into a sense of unity with these persons.

As you come into feeling of union with these persons, know that all beings can be benefactors for one another. We all want to feel this experience of compassionate understanding, love and well-being.

To end this meditation, let yourself rest for a few moments in the peace of things as they are. Just having the wisdom that comes from knowing that you can always be surrounded by the warm compassionate gaze and loving support of benefactors, from your past, your present, and even from those who you may encounter later today or tomorrow.

Lastly, send these benefactors a blessing that reflects your gratitude and appreciation.

Reflections: What was most surprising about this meditation for being *At Peace with Pain*? What benefactors showed up for you?

_____

_____

_____

_____

How did it feel to have compassion for your situation? How did it feeling to be supported by wise and knowing benefactors who understood your pain?

_____

_____

_____

_____

How could this meditation be incorporated into your life? How could it help you to find benefactors or reach out to potential benefactors? How would you go about reaching out or finding these benefactors?

_____

_____

_____

_____

_____

_____

_____

Bibliography/Resources

BOOKS

Altman, Donald, *Art of the Inner Meal: The Power of Mindful Practices to Heal Our Food Cravings*, Moon Lake Media, 2002

Altman, Donald, *A Course in Mindfulness: The Heart of Mindful Living*, Moon Lake Media, 2011 (available at: www.MindfulPractices.com)

Altman, Donald, *Eat, Savor Satisfy: 12-Weeks to Mindful Eating*, Moon Lake Media, 2006 (available at: www.MindfulPractices.com)

Altman, Donald, *The Joy Compass: 8 ways to find lasting happiness, gratitude and optimism in the present moment*, New Harbinger Publications, 2012

Altman, Donald, *Meal by Meal: 365 Daily Meditations for Finding Balance through Mindful Eating*, New World Library, 2004

Altman, Donald, *Living Kindness: The Buddha's Ten Guiding Principles for a Blessed Life*, Moon Lake Media, 2009

Altman, Donald, *Mindfulness Code: Keys for Overcoming Stress, Anxiety, Fear, and Unhappiness*, New World Library, 2010

Altman, Donald, *The Mindfulness Toolbox: 50 Practical Tips, Tools, and Handouts for Anxiety, Depression, Stress, and Pain*, Premier Publishing Media, 2014

Altman, Donald, *One-Minute Mindfulness: 50 Simple Ways to Find Peace, Clarity and New Possibilities in a Stressed Out World*, New World Library, 2011

Altman, Donald, and Crosby, Greg, Chapter 5; *Wiley-Blackwell Handbook of Group Psychotherapy: Integrative Cognitive-Behavioral Group Therapy*, Wiley Books, 2011

Armstrong, Thomas, *7 Kinds of Smart: Identifying and Developing Your Multiple Intelligences*, Plume, 1999

Badenoch, Bonnie, *Being a Brain-Wise Therapist*, W.W.Norton & Co., 2008

Baer, Ruth, *Mindfulness-Based Treatment Approaches*, Elsevier, 2006

Barker, Philip, *Using Metaphors in Psychotherapy*, Bruner Meisel U., 1987

Beck, Judith, *Cognitive Therapy: Basics and Beyond*, Guilford Press, 1995

Begley, Sharon, *Train Your Brain, Change Your Mind*, Ballantine Books, 2007

Benson, Herbert, and Proctor, William, *Relaxation Revolution: The Science and Genetics of Mind Body Healing*, Scribner, 2011

Biswas-Diener, Robert, *Invitation to Positive Psychology: Research and Tools for the Professional*, PositiveAcorn.com, 2008

Bloomquist,H., *Skills Training for Children with Behavior Problems* Guilford Press, 2006

Brantley, Jeffrey. *Calming Your Anxious Mind*, New Harbinger Publications, 2007

Bryant, Fred, and Veroff, Joseph, *Savoring: A New Model of Positive Experience*, Lawrence Erlbaum Associates, 2006

Burns, David, *Feeling Good*, Harper & Row, 1980

Chödrön, Pema, *Start Where You Are: A Guide to Compassionate* Living, Shambala, 2001

Craigie, Jr., Frederic, *Positive Spirituality in Health Care: Nine Practical Approaches to Pursuing Wholeness for Clinicians, Patients, and Health Care Organizations*, Mill City Press, 2010

Daiensai, Richard Kirsten, *Smile: 365 Happy Meditations*, MQ Pub., Ltd., 2004

Davidson, Richard, and Begley, Sharon, *The Emotional Life of Your Brain*, Plume, 2012

Diener, Ed; Biswas-Diener, Robert, *Happiness: Unlocking the Mysteries of Psychological Wealth*, Blackwell Publishing, 2008

Flores, Philip, *Addiction as an Attachment Disorder*, Aronson, 2003

Fralich, Terry, *Cultivating Lasting Happiness*, Premier Publishing Media, 2012

Gershon, Michael, *The Second Brain*, Harper Paperbacks, 1999

Goleman, Daniel, *Destructive Emotions*, Bantam Books, 2003

Gordon, M.D., James, *Unstuck: Your Guide to the Seven-Stage Journey Out of Depression*, Penguin Press, 2008

Groopman, Jerome, *Anatomy of Hope*, Random House, 2005

Hamilton, Allan and Weil, Andrew, *The Scalpel and the Soul*, Tarcher, 2008

Hanson, Rick, *Buddha's Brain: The Practical Neuroscience of Happiness, Love and Wisdom*, New Harbinger Publications, 2009

Hayes, Steven, and Smith, Spencer, *Get Out of Your Mind & Into Your Life*, New Harbinger Publications, 2005

Hayes, Steven; Follette, Victoria; Linehan, Marsha; editors, *Mindfulness and Acceptance: Expanding the Cognitive Behavioral Tradition*, Guilford Press, 2004

Hüther, Gerald, *The Compassionate Brain: How Empathy Creates Intelligence*, Trumpeter Books, 2006

Jevne, R.F., *When Dreams Don't Work: Professional Caregivers and Burnout*, Baywood Publishing Co., 1998

Jevne, R.F. and Miller, J.E., *Finding Hope: Ways to See Life in a Brighter Light*, Willowgreen Publishing, 1999

Kabat-Zinn, Jon, *Full Catastrophe Living: Using the Wisdom of Your Body and Mind to Face Stress, Pain and Illness*, Delacorte Press, 1990

Kabat-Zinn, Jon, *Wherever You Go There You Are: Mindfulness Meditation in Everyday Life*, Hyperion Books, 1997

Kabat-Zinn, Jon and Myla *Everyday Blessings,* Hyperion Books, 1998

Kabat-Zinn, Jon; Teasedale, John; Williams, Mark; Zindel Segal; *The Mindful Way Through Depression*, Guilford Press, 2007

Kaiser Family Foundation. http://kff.org/other/event/generation-m2-media-in-the-lives-of/

Klein, Allen, *The Healing Power of Humor*, Tarcher Press, 1989

Kornfield, Jack, *The Art of Forgiveness, Loving-Kindness, and Peace*, Bantam Books, 2002

Lawley, James & Tompkins, Penny, *Metaphors in Mind: Transformation through Symbolic Modelling*, The Developing Company Press, 2011

Levine, Peter, with Frederick, Ann, *Waking the Tiger: Healing Trauma*, North Atlantic Books, 1997

Linley, Willars, and Biswas-Diener, *The Strengths Book: Be Confident, Be Successful, and Enjoy Better Relationships* by, CAPP Press., 2010

Lyubomirsky, Sonja, *The How of Happiness*, Penguin, 2008

Marra, T, *Depressed & Anxious: The Dialectical Behavioral Therapy Workbook for Overcoming Depression and Anxiety*, New Harbinger Publications, 2004

Martin, Kathleen, Ed., *The Book of Symbols*, Taschen, Germany, 2010

McDermott, Diane, *Making Hope Happen,* New Harbinger Publications, 1999

McDermott, Diane., and Snyder, C.R., *The Great Big Book of Hope*, New Harbinger Publications, 2000

Mehl-Madrona, Lewis, *Healing the Mind through the Power of Story*, Bear and Co., 2010

Merzenich, Michael, *Soft-Wired: How the New Science of Brain Plasticity Can Change Your Life*, Parnassus Publishing, 2013

Mikulincer, Mario., and Shaver, Philip, *Attachment in Adulthood*, Guilford Press, 2007

Najavits, Lisa, *Seeking Safety*, Guilford Press, 2001

Naperstek, Bellruth, *Staying Well with Guided Imagery*, Warner Books, 1994

O'Connor, Richard, *Undoing Perpetual Stress*, Berkley Trade Books, 2006

O'Donohue, John, *Anam Cara: A Book of Celtic Wisdom*, Harper Perennial, 1998

Padesky, C. A., & Greenberger, D., *Clinician's Guide to Mind Over Mood*. Guilford Press, 1995

Ratey, James, *Spark: The Revolutionary New Science of Exercise and the Brain*, Little, Brown, and Co., 2008

Salzberg, Sharon, *Loving Kindness: The Revolutionary Art of Happiness*, Shambala, 1995

Sapolsky, Robert, *Why Zebras Don't Get Ulcers*, W.H. Freeman and Co., 1994

Schwartz and Gladding, *You Are Not Your Brain*, Avery Publishing, 2011

Schwartz, Jeffrey, *Brain Lock*, Harper Perennial, 1996

Schwartz, Jeffrey, and Begley, Sharon, *The Mind and the Brain: Neuroplasticity and the Power of Mental Force*, ReganBooks, 2003

Segal, Z.V., Williams, J., Mark, G., & Teasdale, J. D., *Mindfulness-Based Cognitive Therapy for depression*, Guilford Press, 2002

Segal, Zindel; Williams, Mark; Teasdale, John, *Mindfulness-Based Cognitive Therapy for Depression*, Guilford Press, 2002

Seligman, Martin, *Learned Optimism*, Vintage Publishers, 2006

Shedon & Kasdan & Steger, editors, *Designing Positive Psychology*, Oxford University Press, 2011

Siegel, Dan, *The Developing Mind*, Guilford Press, 2012

Siegel, Dan, and Hartzell, *Parenting From the inside Out*, Tarcher Books, 2003

Siegel, Dan, and Payne Bryson, Tina, *The Whole Brain Child*, Bantam Books, 2012

Silananda, U., *The Four Foundations of Mindfulness*, Wisdom Publications, 2003

Snyder, C.R., *The Handbook of Hope*, Academic Press, 2000

Snyder, C.R., *The Psychology of Hope*, Free Press, 2003

Snyder, C.R., McDermott, Cook, and Rapoff, *Hope for the Journey: Helping Children Through Good Times and Bad*, Basic Books, 1997

Snyder, C.R. and Ford, C., *Coping with Negative Life Events*, Springer, 1987

Somov, Pavel, *Anger Management Jumpstart: A 4-Session Mindfulness Path to Compassion and Change*, PESI Publishing & Media, 2013

Somov, Pavel, *Present Perfect: A Mindfulness Approach to Letting Go of Perfectionism and the Need for Control*, New Harbinger Publications, 2010

Tarragona, Margarita, *Positive Identities: Narrative Practices and Positive Psychology*, PositiveAcorn. com, 2012

Thich Nhat Hanh, *The Miracle of Mindfulness*, Beacon Press, 1976

Wehrenberg, Margaret, *The 10 Best-Ever Anxiety Management Techniques*, W.W. Norton & Co., 2008

Whybrow, Peter, *American Mania: When More Is Not Enough*, W.W.Norton & Co., 2006

WEBSITES

Donald Altman'sBooks and Guided Meditation CDs:
www.MindfulPractices.com
www.TheJoyCompass.com
www.OneMinuteMindfulnessBook.com
www.MindfulnessCode.Com

Center for Investigating Healthy Minds:
www.investigatinghealthyminds.org

Center for Mindful Eating:
www.TCME.org

Dana Foundation Brain and Immunology Newsletter:
www.dana.org

Forgiveness Project:
www.theforgivenessproject.com

Global Association for Interpersonal Neurobiology Studies:
www.mindgains.org

Greater Good Science Center:
www.greatergood.berkeley.edu

Hope Foundation, for Educators:
www.hopefoundation.org

Humor Project:
www.thehumorproject.com

Laughter Heals Foundation:
www.laughterheals.org

Laughter Yoga International:
www.laughteryoga.org

Mindful Awareness Research Center:
www.marc.ucla.edu

Mindfulness Research Monthly:
www.mindfulexperience.org

Mind & Life Institute:
www.mindandlife.org

Music and Happiness:
> www.musicandhappiness.com

Network for Grateful Living:
> www.gratefulness.org

Optimist International:
> www.optimist.org

Scientific American Mind:
> www.SciAmMind.com

Social Cognitive Neuroscience Laboratory, UCLA:
> www.scn.ucla.edu

For your convenience, we have established a dedicated website to download all the worksheets and exercises. This gives you a choice to photocopy from the book or printing

go.pesi.com/Mindfulnesstoolbox

Index

Made in the USA
Middletown, DE
28 September 2020